Essex
Edited by Steve Twelvetree

First published in Great Britain in 2005 by:
Young Writers
Remus House
Coltsfoot Drive
Peterborough
PE2 9JX
Telephone: 01733 890066
Website: www.youngwriters.co.uk

All Rights Reserved

© *Copyright Contributors 2005*

SB ISBN 1 84602 160 X

Foreword

Young Writers was established in 1991 and has been passionately devoted to the promotion of reading and writing in children and young adults ever since. The quest continues today. Young Writers remains as committed to the fostering of burgeoning poetic and literary talent as ever.

This year's Young Writers competition has proven as vibrant and dynamic as ever and we are delighted to present a showcase of the best poetry from across the UK. Each poem has been carefully selected from a wealth of *Playground Poets* entries before ultimately being published in this, our thirteenth primary school poetry series.

Once again, we have been supremely impressed by the overall high quality of the entries we have received. The imagination, energy and creativity which has gone into each young writer's entry made choosing the best poems a challenging and often difficult but ultimately hugely rewarding task - the general high standard of the work submitted amply vindicating this opportunity to bring their poetry to a larger appreciative audience.

We sincerely hope you are pleased with our final selection and that you will enjoy *Playground Poets Essex* for many years to come.

Contents

Debden CE Primary School
Amelia James-Phillips (8)	1
Olivia Doust (8)	2
Katie Hill (8)	3
Dan Gough (11)	3
Thomas Gair (8)	4
David Ross-Adams (9)	4
John Clark (8)	5
Lucy Manuel (7)	5
Conor McCahill (7)	6
Alex Francis (8)	6
Phoebe Lindsell (7)	7
Freya Robb (7)	7
Abbie Stevens (10)	8
Caitlin Harding (9)	8
Jennifer van Hees (10)	9
Dorothy Hughes (8)	9
Felicity Lawrie (10)	10
Eva James-Phillips (8)	10
Eleanor Tew (8)	11
Fred Haselton (10)	11
Josh Manuel (9)	11
Katie Clark (11)	12
Matilda Hughes (10)	12
Alex Forbes (11)	13
Tom Read (10)	13
Billy Dixon (8)	14
Polly Oakman (10)	14
Daniel Clarke (9)	14
Robert Barber (11)	15
Dominic Burchall (9)	15
Michael Pearce (10)	16
Theodore Bozzi-Catlin (9)	16
Alice Hughes (10)	17
Amie Roper (10)	17
Emily Patterson (11)	18
Lauren Tsitsaros (11)	18

Fairlop Primary School
    Maya Owen (10)   19

Fingringhoe CE Primary School
    April Podd (10)   21
    Michaela Bartholomew (9)   22
    Aimee Salmon (10)   23
    Sam Francis (11)   24
    Liam Clewley (11)   25
    Rosina Turner (10)   26
    Philippa O'Toole (10)   27

Great Bardfield Primary School
    Sacha Jones (8)   27
    Joe Clark (9)   28
    Maggie Cooper (9)   28
    Dominic Baines (9)   29
    George Stephens (9)   29
    Marielle Dorset (8)   30
    Harris Churchman (8)   30
    Ollie Bedding (10)   31
    Natasha Jones (8)   31
    Helena Terry (9)   32
    Georgina Bray (10)   32
    Laura Graham (9)   33
    Cam Meldrum (11)   34
    Katie Rees (10)   35
    Eleanor Jones (9)   36
    India Witham (10)   37
    Stacey Gibson (10)   38

Great Bradfords Junior School
    Cameron Ayling (9)   38
    Ji Young Lee (9)   39
    Rhys Kelly (9)   39
    Samuel Stedman (9)   40
    Matthew Horne (10)   41
    Alexandra Jenkins (9)   41
    Dominick Wiseman (9)   42
    Larissa Clarke (10)   42
    Adam Pillinger (9)   43

Ryan Cheek (9)	43
Carly Ellis (9)	44
Lucy Norwood (10)	44
Jamie Copus (9)	45
Ellis Graham (10)	45
Shaun Whiteley (10)	45
Amie Blackburn (9)	46
Darren Brown (9)	46
Joanna Bray (9)	47
Rebecca Collar (9)	47
Jedariah Noble-Hull (9)	48
Alexander Newman (10)	48
Abbie Green (9)	49
Maria Thomas (9)	49
Abbie Pillet (10)	50
Ryan Sycamore (10)	50
William Stephens (9)	51
Stephanie Turner (9)	51
Rosie Irons (10)	52
Nathan Gypps (10)	52
Alex Miller (9)	52
Micah Salmon (9)	53
Sophie Bass (9)	53
Keren Pegg (10)	53
Charlie Schofield (10)	54
Paul Saunders (9)	54
Adam Sharman (10)	55
Megan Craig (10)	55
Lucy Ogan (10)	56
Bronwyn Morley (9)	56
Nia Griffiths (10)	57
Ben Phillips (10)	57
Zoe Soraf (9)	58
Kieran Notley (9)	58
Owen Hoare (10)	58

Holland Park Primary School

Danny Christie (10)	59
Alex Cox (11)	59
Ava Pickett (11)	60
Nicky Fillingham (7)	60

Georgia Hickey (10)	61
Madeline Allis (8)	61
Megan Steel (11)	62
Hannah Munford (10)	62
Bethany Godwin (9)	63
Tyler Rendell (10)	63
Liam Torr-Clark (10)	64
Jasmine Swinbourne (11)	64
Jasmine Allen (11)	65
Katie Herbert (10)	65
Bradley R Hackett (11)	66
Christopher Gadeke (11)	66
Gemma Gardiner (10)	67
Max Gage (10)	67
Matthew Illsley (10)	68
Chloe Nicholson (11)	68
Megan Larkins (8)	69
Paige Dawson (8)	69
Nancy Sword (8)	69
Isabella Roberts (10)	70
Millie Adler (8)	71
Amber Will (8)	71
Holly Childerley (9)	72
Toms George (9)	72
Ryan Day (10)	73
Hannah Harvey (9)	73
Ellen Gage (11)	74
Charley Manners (10)	75
Brea Blundell (9)	75
Ryan Croke (10)	76
Christopher Ashdown (11)	76
Gemma Day (10)	77
Gaby Baldock (11)	77
David Sayer (11)	78
Grace Barlow (10)	78
Kirsty Muir	78
Chelsea Hindley (10)	79
Amber Watts (10)	79
Rebecca Hoffman (11)	80
Tom Childerley (11)	80
Kyle Lowis (11)	81
Emily Hills (9)	81

Lydia Waller (10)	82
James Bettis (11)	82
Ami Fosker (8)	83
Clare Gravatt (10)	83
Charlotte Batchelor (10)	83
Loren Janes (10)	84
Katherine Langdon (11)	84
Anya Klarner (10)	85
Ieuan Gledhill (10)	85
Amy Wright (11)	86
Samantha Pinches (11)	86
Shannan Weeks (10)	87
Sarah Watson (10)	87
Harry Ryan (10)	88
Tom Wilkinson (10)	88
Robyn Clemenson (8)	89
Mikey Irving (8)	89
Rachel Clark (8)	90
Georgia Humphries (9)	90
Gabrielle Shaw (11)	91
Robyn Wiggins (9)	91
Sean Hobbins (8)	91
Bradley Reeve (8)	92
Sasha Leatherbarrow (10)	92
Terry Baker (9)	93

Holy Family RC Primary School

Amelia Jardine	94

Mayflower Primary School

Thomas Kemp (9)	94
Rebecca Lauder (10)	95
Lucy Young (10)	95
Erin Carman (9)	96
Amy Farrington (11)	96
James Macdonald (10)	97
Jordan Heath (10)	97
Alex Chapman (11)	98
Bethany Starkings (10)	98
Matthew Swallow (10)	99
Georgia Houghton (10)	100

Laura Green (10)	100
Sabrina Parsons (10)	101
Abbie Elwood (10)	101
Eleanor Proctor (11)	102
Joanna Shields (11)	102
Georgia Howell (11)	103
Jack Copping (10)	103
Peter Howell (9)	104
Daryl Whiffing (10)	104
Ryan Heath (10)	105
Naomi Edgar (11)	105
Sophie Scott (10)	106
Thomas Denney (10)	106
Paisley Tedder (10)	107
Tiger Love (11)	107
Jemma Free (10)	108
Ben Tedder (10)	108
Callum Miller (10)	108
Lloyd Beeney (11)	109
Kelly Chatterton (11)	110
Amelia Gooding (10)	110
Yasmeen Amber (9)	111
Bethany Slater (10)	111
Hayley Walker (10)	111
Jordan Rodger (9)	112
Hannah Coleman (10)	113
Kiana Knight (10)	113
Jade Paice (10)	113
Max Garnier (11)	114
Tom Goldsmith (11)	115

Parsons Heath CE Primary School

Emma Smith (10)	116
Charlotte Holmes & George Clarke (11)	117
Charlotte Chubb (10)	118
Jack McKenna (10)	118
Kelvin Yeung (11)	119
Mitchell Attwood (11)	119
Aidan Ware (10)	120
Alice Byford (10)	120
Jamie Boughton (11)	121

Alex Partridge (11)	121
Emily Townsend (10)	122
Bradley Orr (10)	122
Rosie Watts (10)	123
Sophie Davies (10)	123
Joshua Goodings (10)	124
Evie Bolderson (11)	125
Paul Byford (10)	126

R A Butler Junior School

Alicia Foley (11)	126
Ella Hampson (11)	127
Sam Sawtell (10)	127
Caitlin Jackson Corbett (11)	128
Rebecca Watts (10)	129
Alice Bol (10)	130
Trudi Saunders (10)	131
Ned Harvey (10)	132
Tom Carruthers (10)	132
Anna Dodge (10)	133
Emma Jenkins (11)	134
Eddie Pottrill (10)	135
Lizzie Clark (10)	136
Oliver Moktar (10)	136
Harry Stocking (10)	137
Jenny King (10)	137
Emily Bayford (10)	138
Anthony Waite (10)	138
Fraser Parry (10)	139
Emily Smith (11)	139
Jai Goodwin (11)	140
Zoë Maskell (11)	141
Morgan Brooks (10)	142
Julia Marsden (10)	143
Alice Marks (10)	144
Oliver Gramlick (10)	144
Lucy Breed (11)	145
Tom Wass (11)	146
Nick Fane (10)	147
Danny Elstub (11)	148
Ryan Martin (10)	149

Zoë Lett (11)   150
William Lockton (10)   151

St Andrew's CE Primary School, North Weald
Lizzie Bailey (8)   151
Kaylee Orchard (10)   152
Jason Caffrey (9)   152
Thomas Southgate (10)   152
George Sykes (10)   153
Lacey Marie Payton (11)   153
Kelly White (10)   153
Charlie Holloway (10)   154
Lauren Barrett (10)   154
Tillie Merritt (9)   155
Samantha Gallacher-Bright (8)   155
Emily Thomasz (7)   156
Lauren Huff (8)   156
Jack Holloway (8)   157
Daniel Neat (9)   157
Lewis Sibley (10)   158
Alec Pike (9)   158
Luke Carrington (10)   158
James Gomez (8)   159
Daniel Gooderham (8)   159
Jack Osborne (8)   159
Jamie Fall (8)   160
Amy Mohr (9)   160
Charlotte Levy (9)   161
Beth Sibley (9)   161
Jordan Albert (8)   161
Rebecca Wheeler (9)   162
Rebecca Cole (8)   162
Adam Berwick (8)   162
Katie Mehew (9)   163
David Paterson (9)   163
Lucy-Ann Phillips (9)   163
Daniel Mallett (9)   164
Eloise White (9)   164
Lee Goody (9)   164
Stevie Smithson (9)   165
Alfie Russell (9)   165

Reece Donoghue (9)	165
Sam Berwick (9)	166
Matthew Wheatley (9)	166
Ben Warren (9)	166
Scarlett Stock (8)	167
Charlotte Jones (9)	167
Thomas Saye (9)	167
Ben Bailey (8)	168
Chloe West (8)	168
Harry Docking (8)	168
Jordan Smith (7)	169
Lewis King (10)	169
Richard Bailey (7)	169
Amy Morris (8)	170
Sam Barker (10)	170

St Teresa's RC Primary School, Colchester

Iona Manley (9)	171
Daniel O'Reilly (9)	171
Glenn Wheeler (9)	172
Anna Bishop (9)	172
Alfie Payne (9)	173
Charyl Spencer (10)	173
Conor Culhane (10)	173
Keshini Gooneratne (10)	174
Ben Brown (10)	174
Daniel Congdon (9)	175
Abigail Payne (9)	175
John Deasy (10)	176
Katie Clements (9)	176
Jack Lugar (9)	176
Alex Partner (10)	177
Paola Williams (9)	177
Ruth Chanarin (9)	177
Rachel Cresswell (9)	178
Bradley Collins (10)	178
Christine Quilty (10)	179
Benjamin Woods (10)	179
Chloe Williams (10)	180
William Jennings (10)	181
Rebecca Lenihan (10)	181

Joe Campe (9)	182
Nicollas Campbell (9)	182
James Chambers (9)	183
Sophie Wilcocks (9)	183

The Daiglen School

Ryan Jackson (10)	183
Jacob Hopkins (10)	184
Jason Chan (10)	184
Sam Winter (11)	184
Sam Dooley (10)	185
Max Goreham (8)	185
Roshan Sukeerathan (10)	185
Connor Marcelis (8)	186
Chirage Valera (10)	186
Charlie Pigrome (8)	186
Nigel Ip (10)	187
Jake Lewis (7)	187
Samuel Meah (8)	188
Harrison Jones (8)	188
Zain Rana (7)	189
Joe Garland (8)	189
Ali Siddiqui (10)	189

Tolleshunt D'Arcy St Nicholas CE Primary School

William Reynolds (10)	190
Zoe Rigby (9)	190
Josh Bolding (11)	191
Grace Goodman (9)	191
Clare Lofthouse (8)	192
Harry Wakefield (8)	192
Ryan Bentley (8)	192
Chloe Double (8)	193
James Baker (9)	193
Tom Delderfield (8)	193
Sarah Harris (8)	194
Jessica Poulter (9)	194
William Skelton (9)	194
Sam Armstrong (11)	195
Sarah King (7)	195
George Basham (9)	195

Alice Moore (7)	196
Emmie Bolding (8)	196
Maya Tucker (9)	196
Kristie Smith (9)	197
Drew Talbot (9)	197
George Davison (7)	197
Amy Harrison (9)	198
Ashley Hawkes (9)	198
Christopher Lewis (8)	198
Katie Lofthouse (11)	199
Brendan Bush (7)	199
Ben Rees (9)	199
Edward Baker (7)	200
Katie Peaker (7)	200
Amy Hawkes (7)	200
Jack Garrett (7)	200
Kelly Bentley (7)	201
Sam Harris (8)	201
Alice Pettican (8)	201
Stacey Dolby (8)	201
Joshua Searles (7)	202
India Rigby (7)	202
Frederick Phillips (8)	202
Ben Knights (10)	203
Summer Phillips (10)	203
Adam Dyster (11)	204

The Poems

The Rainforest

Slowly and silently, the sun creeps up the sky.
Golden beams flash all around.
The sun is like a gold nugget,
Thrown so high,
It will not come down.
The sky is like a shimmering ruby,
Glowing red above all the towering trees.
A bright mist hangs from the air,
Like a gleaming and glowing sheet of silver glitter.
The sun glows stronger and stronger,
Until it forces the mist to evaporate,
And then to disappear altogether.
All the animals creep out of their homes,
They are greeted by a dazzling sun.
The crickets croak as they scavenge for something to drink.

All is quiet over the steamy rainforest.
The only sound is the secretive rustling of leaves.
The silence is shattered!
Thunder booms!
Lightning flashes!
Trees sway, leaves fall to the ground,
And that is where they lay.
The sky glows with light.
The wind flows just like water,
Making the trees brush madly against the sky.
The lightning is flashing closer to the trees,
Threatening to snap them into many pieces.
Thunder booms like a rolling drum.
Trees are rolling, closer and closer they come!

Amelia James-Phillips (8)
Debden CE Primary School

I'd Rather Be . . .

I'd rather be a snake than a mouse.
I'd rather be a cottage than a house.
I'd rather be a bush than a flower.
I'd rather be a minute than an hour.
I'd rather be a stripe than a spot.
I'd rather be a cat than a dog.
I'd rather be clean than dirty.
I'd rather be hungry than thirsty.
I'd rather be in China than Japan.
I'd rather be a woman than a man.
I'd rather be the sun than a rainbow.
I'd rather be a mountain than a volcano.
I'd rather be right than wrong.
I'd rather be a bell than a gong.
I'd rather be water than food.
I'd rather be happy than in a mood.
I'd rather be a table than a chair.
I'd rather be a human than a bear.
I'd rather be an elephant than its trunk.
I'd rather be a normal human than a punk.
I'd rather be a lion than a cat.
I'd rather be a scarf than a hat.
I'd rather be a bush than a tree.
I'd rather be a wasp than a bee.
I'd rather be a lorry than a car.
I'd rather be near than far.
I'd rather be the sand than the sea.
I'd rather be you than me.
I'd rather be a tap than a sink.
I'd rather be a blink than a wink.

Olivia Doust (8)
Debden CE Primary School

The Rainforest

The sun rises into the sky.
The sun starts to peep over the trees.
The light cracks open.
The beams fire like golden flames.
The sun dazzles.
The mist starts to burn away and fade.
The animals scurry across the ground
                            for shade and water and food.
The water drops are like a drooling, dribbling mouth.

The rainforest is a hot, sticky, misty place.
Morning, it is sunny, hot, sweaty and steamy.
Night, it is dark, stormy, wet, damp
And the clouds are black and puffy.
The rain is like a bubbling fish tank.
The thunder is like a roaring, booming,
                            raging, shattering piece of glass.
The vines are like a tangling knot.
The leaves are shiny, rich green flapping leaves.
The monkeys are shouting and screaming.
The poisonous snakes hiss across the ground.
The birds tweet like a flute playing.

Katie Hill (8)
Debden CE Primary School

Gregory Grasshopper

Hopping, skipping, doing a jig,
Onto the grass, onto the shed,
Lanky legs that bend then throw,
Onto the flowers, onto the stone,
Clicking limbs that make a racket,
Onto the hedge, onto the window,
Aiming feelers then off we go!

Dan Gough (11)
Debden CE Primary School

I'd Rather Be . . .

I'd rather be north than south.
I'd rather be teeth than a mouth.
I'd rather be east than west.
I'd rather be exhausted than at rest.
I'd rather be up than down.
I'd rather be a village than a town.
I'd rather be yes than no.
I'd rather be an eagle than a crow.
I'd rather be a bird than a worm.
I'd rather be a year than a term.
I'd rather be a ponytail than a bun.
I'd rather be a gram than a tonne.
I'd rather be a wasp than a bee.
I'd rather be a dwarf than me.
I'd rather be happy than sad.
I'd rather be good than bad.
I'd rather be sea than land.
I'd rather be a circus than a band.
I'd rather be a cow than a lamb.
I'd rather be pork than ham.
I'd rather be baseball than cricket.
I'd rather be a note than a ticket.
I'd rather be a minute than an hour.
I'd rather be a palace than a tower.
I'd rather be a cottage than a house.
I'd rather be a cat than a mouse.

Thomas Gair (8)
Debden CE Primary School

Rainforest

Dawn in the rainforest.
The hazy sun pokes through the mist
The animals wake, ready to kill and eat.

David Ross-Adams (9)
Debden CE Primary School

The Rainforest

Dawn in the rainforest.
The sun is rising.
The sun is as red as blood.
It sparkles like gold and silver.
The mist wraps around the trees
Like long ribbons.
The animals scurry for shade.
The sun burns the mist away.

Over the steamy rainforest
Thick, black, towering clouds fill the sky.
Raging, roaring, booming
Thunder rumbles across the sky.
Shattering, crackling lightning,
Travels at the speed of a jumbo jet.
The rain pitter-patters on,
The leaves like footsteps on the ground.
When the torrential rain comes
The rain falls like bullets being shot out of the clouds.

John Clark (8)
Debden CE Primary School

Rainforest Storm

Wind blowing, clouds growing
Lightning crackling, trees swaying
Howling monkeys all over the rainforest
All the other animals are scurrying for shelter
The rain swirls and falls off the shiny leaves
The leaves sparkle like diamonds.

Lucy Manuel (7)
Debden CE Primary School

The Rainforest

The rainforest is dark.
The sun peeps up from the horizon.
The beautiful sun shows its smile.
The swirling mist wraps itself around the forest.
The water dribbles like a drooling mouth.
The sun gets higher.
The mist gets burnt away.
Blinding beams of light cover the rainforest.
Roaring, rumbling,
Raging clouds gliding across sky.
Booming black thunder.
Crashing lightning like smashing glass.
Crackling lightning like sparklers.
Forks of lightning like spurts of fire.
Rich green leaves.
Torrential rain like a hurricane.

Conor McCahill (7)
Debden CE Primary School

The Rainforest

The bright, shining, golden sun rising,
Clearing the sky of the blurry, grey mist.
Birds singing to each other.
The sun is as gold as a big, shining door handle.
The mist is wrapping round the trees like silver ribbons.
Water dripping into its stream.
Big, bushy, nimbus clouds spitting down diamond raindrops.
Raindrops getting heavier and heavier,
Falling even faster than before.
All of a sudden you hear thumping thunder.
You see a speeding flash of lightning in the air.
The thunder gets louder and the lightning gets lower.

Alex Francis (8)
Debden CE Primary School

The Rainforest

The sun shone like dazzling golden butter.
It filled up the forest with golden lights like on a Christmas tree.
The mist came.
The mist looked like murky water.
It wrapped its cosy blanket around the forest.
Crackling crickets jumped about like someone on a trampoline.
The sun shone blindly.
A storm came whirling, twirling about.
Deep, terrifying clombus clouds whirled about.
Crashing, banging noises
Then the thunder came.
It sounded like shattering glass.
It was towering above the trees.
The rain fell, it dived and scattered onto the floor.
The leaves held a lot of rain.

Phoebe Lindsell (7)
Debden CE Primary School

The Rainforest

The sun is rising
The sky is like a blood-red party frock
The sun is like a bright yellow ball in the sky
The rain tiptoeing then stamping
Then falling like cannonballs.

Damp, fluffy, trembling
Crashing, bashing, cold, wet
Black, thundering
Pitter-patter lightning, like fireworks
Is a bolt of light
There is a splattering.

Freya Robb (7)
Debden CE Primary School

Through That Door
(Inspired by 'Through That Door' by John Cotton)

Through that door,
Is a secret room,
Dark and spooky
And some gloom.

Through that door,
Is the ocean shore,
A bright orange crab
Crawling on the floor.

Through that door
Is a red wall,
Someone sitting,
Someone falls.

Through that door,
Is a waterfall,
Bashing and crashing
You can't hear the birds call!

Abbie Stevens (10)
Debden CE Primary School

Through That Door
(Inspired by 'Through That Door' by John Cotton)

Through that door,
There's a river in my mind,
Where all thoughts flow and tumble,
Leaving all reasons to stay here far behind.

Caitlin Harding (9)
Debden CE Primary School

Jimbob

He's sillier then mental old Polly,
But not at all like a freaky dolly,
He's softer than a baby's bum,
He likes to eat codfish gum,
He's fatter than a hippopotamus,
His cousin is a flippinotomus,
His arms are like the branches of a willow,
He's fluffier than a fluffy pillow,
He's hairier than a hairy head,
His favourite colour is blood-red,
He's happier than the birthday girls,
He goes to the toilet then he hurls,
He's louder than a dinosaur's roar,
He has one tiny little paw,
He's red, blue, green
His breed's Mageen
And his name is . . . *Jimbob!*

Jennifer van Hees (10)
Debden CE Primary School

I'd Rather Be . . .

I'd rather be a fence than a wall
I'd rather be a hoop than a ball
I'd rather be a snake than a mouse
I'd rather be a cottage than a house
I'd rather be a president than a pirate
I'd rather be a spade than a bucket
I'd rather be a book than a bag
I'd rather be happy than sad
I'd rather be a table than a chair
I'd rather be a person than a bear
I'd rather be a mountain than a volcano
I'd rather be yes than no.

Dorothy Hughes (8)
Debden CE Primary School

Four Seasons

Winter sat down and put his gloves on
And took a deep breath
Then opened the door
And entered the cold.

Summer danced across the field
Looking at the clear blue sky
As the warm wind washed past her.

Spring jumped out of her bed
And hurried downstairs
Then stopped and closed her eyes
Then opened the door
To turn the world warm again.

Autumn ran down the path
Kicking the leaves at the same time.
Then stopped to pick some conkers
And carried on home.

Felicity Lawrie (10)
Debden CE Primary School

I'd Rather Be . . .

I'd rather be first than last.
I'd rather be a shark than a fish.
I'd rather be slow than fast.
I'd rather be soup than the dish.
I'd rather be scissors than paper.
I'd rather be a lid than a pen.
I'd rather have things now than later.
I'd rather be nine than ten.
I'd rather be happy than grumpy.
I'd rather be covered than bare.
I'd rather be smooth than lumpy.
I'd rather be common than rare.

Eva James-Phillips (8)
Debden CE Primary School

Rainforest

The sun rises with a blinding beam of golden flames
While the mist is calling out animal names
Dazzling spears of blood-red sunlight fill the sky
A dribbling mouse and a very slow sloth
While a jaguar's mouth is filling with froth
Birds are singing melodies, the crickets are croaking
While howler monkeys are choking
Over the steamy forest the rain is falling
The lightning is crackling, then with one almighty crash
Like a bolt from the blue a spurt of fire bolts from the clouds.

Eleanor Tew (8)
Debden CE Primary School

Through That Door
(Inspired by 'Through That Door' by John Cotton)

Through that door,
Is a jungle in my mind,
Where I can play around,
It's a place that I can find.

Over that mountain,
Are animals big and small,
Listen closely
And you will hear birds make their calls.

Fred Haselton (10)
Debden CE Primary School

Anger

Anger is crimson
It smells like a hot iron smouldering,
Anger tastes burnt and bitter,
It sounds like teeth grinding together,
It feels hard and sharp,
Anger lives in the heart of a volcano.

Josh Manuel (9)
Debden CE Primary School

Somewhere In The World Today

Somewhere in the world today . . .
a salmon is violently flinging itself
up a wonderful waterfall.

Somewhere in the world today . . .
rabbits are playfully fighting happily.

Somewhere in the world today . . .
a hunter shouts at a harmless bird
flying innocently over the trees.

Somewhere in the world today . . .
a tiger quietly creeps
towards a delicious dinner of antelope.

Somewhere in the world today . . .
a squid frantically squeezes his black ink
out of his jelly-like body.

Katie Clark (11)
Debden CE Primary School

The Seasons

Spring was shedding off her winter clothes
as she danced round the fields dropping petals at her feet.

Summer's eyes were glowing brightly
as she paddled in the blue glittering sea.

Autumn was walking round gardens
picking fruit and berries for harvest,
dropping leaves, turning them gold, leaving the trees bare for winter.

Winter was playing in the snow collecting icicles and snowflakes
to make Christmas decorations.

Matilda Hughes (10)
Debden CE Primary School

Lost Property

I looked into that plastic box,
To see what I could see,
There's a range of different people's clothes,
But no shorts for PE!
There's . . .
Duncan's spare lunchbox,
Robert's long trousers,
Dan's hockey kit,
Katie's many blouses,
Ella's long, shiny boot,
Emily's new fleece
And Amie's old broken flute.
It's all shiny, like it's been in grease!
Inside that old red box there's . . .
Aha! Shorts, whoopee!
Red and short and stretched,
I wonder if they'll fit me?

Alex Forbes (11)
Debden CE Primary School

Lost Property

I looked into the plastic box,
To see what I could see,
Isn't that Dan's hat that he lost last week?
And isn't that Duncan's lunchbox,
He was trying to seek?
Hey, that's my top I tried to find,
I really had to use my mind.
Lost property I do hate,
Just because I can never find any of my stuff.
Aren't they Mrs Mitchell's glasses on the floor?
Mrs Mitchell must feel so poor.

Tom Read (10)
Debden CE Primary School

The Rainforest

The morning mist begins to vanish as the sun peeks out
The monkeys swing from tree to tree making a howling noise
Snakes slither through the leaves
The rivers meet at the edge of the forest.

The forest is calm
Then a storm comes along
With great big black clouds
Thunder and lightning
Animals go to the safest place
Then the storm is over.

Billy Dixon (8)
Debden CE Primary School

Dartmoor Pony

A Dartmoor pony with heavy feet
A plaited mane, ever so neat
Silky fur going one way
Talking to each other with a soft neigh
To and fro the tail goes
Brushing against their hairy toes
Cantering across a grassy plain
The wind whistling through their long manes.

Polly Oakman (10)
Debden CE Primary School

Misery

Misery is misty grey,
It smells like black, puffy smoke,
Misery tastes sharp and strong,
It sounds like sighing on a rainy day,
It feels like a rusty, blunt sword,
Misery lives in the heart of a damp, dark fog.

Daniel Clarke (9)
Debden CE Primary School

My Pet

I have a two-headed hippo named Morris
And he sleeps in my bed.
And when he snores
He sprays spit on my head.

He eats a lot of food
And sucks it up like a hoover.
When we put him on scales
He weighed more than Vancouver.

And when he has gas
It's a terrible sight.
Green stuff comes out of his behind
And people run in fright.

When we went to London,
He made a new mate.
He made McDonald's close down
And got stuck in Traitors Gate.

My hippo got food poisoning,
We had to put him to sleep,
His grave was a mile wide
And twenty-five miles deep.

Robert Barber (11)
Debden CE Primary School

Over That Mountain
(Inspired by 'Through That Door' by John Cotton)

Over that mountain,
Is a mighty waterfall,
Which towers over everything,
Over 20 metres tall.

Over that mountain,
Is the river of my mind,
It thrashes down,
Leaving all that's bad behind.

Dominic Burchall (9)
Debden CE Primary School

Mika

Mika spins and spins,
Knocks over bins,
He eats and chews
And eats my stews,
He is just fine,
Except for spilling wine.
He is tired and lazy
But can get crazy.
When people come past,
He jumps up fast.
He loves to go on runs,
But he also loves chocolate buns.
His teeth are going black,
But that doesn't stop him
Eating the shoe rack.

Michael Pearce (10)
Debden CE Primary School

Through That Door
(Inspired by 'Through That Door' by John Cotton)

Through that door a magical mind lies.
Conjuring and mixing through many eyes.

When you open the door it is colourful
And hypnotising and full of scares.

There is a cooling and waxing and wailing like the moon.
Witch glares through your starry and twinkly eyes.

A derelict building stands in front of you
Like a splashing wave willing to go further on.

Look at it, look at it through the mist.
Fading away like a startled shimmer.

Theodore Bozzi-Catlin (9)
Debden CE Primary School

Thing

Furry as a lion's mane,
Faster than an underground train.
Fur as dark as ebony,
Fun and joy for you and me.
Eyes as blue as the sky,
He's very tall and he can fly.
Happier than a bumblebee,
Likes to play by the sea.
Louder than an aeroplane about to fly,
Doesn't stop playing from morning to nigh.
Fiercer than a daisy,
He's very, very lazy.
Funnier than a clown,
Likes to walk down to town.
He likes to bake chocolate cake
And makes his own mini lake.

Alice Hughes (10)
Debden CE Primary School

Thing

Taller than the tallest tree,
Older than the world can be,
Smaller than the smallest mouse,
Bigger than the biggest house,
Smellier than a smelly sock,
Slower than the ticking clock,
Louder than a roaring lion,
Quieter than the snail - Brian,
Faster than the running hare,
Kinder than the kindest mare,

That's my thing!

Amie Roper (10)
Debden CE Primary School

Limericks

There was a young lady called Marth
Who loved a jolly good laugh.
She wriggled her toes
And twitched her nose
And enjoyed a big bubbly bath.

There was a young man from Spain
Who loved to dance in the rain
He caught a bad cold
And then turned bald
And found he was quite insane.

There was a boy called Lars
Who liked to play with cars
He beeped the horn
And drove till dawn
And then discovered Mars.

Emily Patterson (11)
Debden CE Primary School

The Four Seasons

Spring dances round the garden,
Surrounded by glowing daffodils.

Summer turns up the heat button,
Allowing the sun to beam down on the colourful flowers.

Autumn walks through the golden brown leaves,
Joyfully kicking them with her feet.

Winter looks through the frosted glass
To see her garden covered in a sheet of white snow.

Lauren Tsitsaros (11)
Debden CE Primary School

Them

I walk out of the classroom
Smell the fresh air
Then I remember

   Them

I don't know when it's going to happen
I don't know when
I don't know why
I really don't think they care
They never care

   Them

I can't tell anyone
I don't know what would happen if I did
It would probably make it worse though
That's why I can't tell
I've just got to go through with it
Maybe it doesn't matter
I expect it
Every day

   Them

I try to run
But I can't
I try to shout
But I can't
My feet are glued
I'm frozen

I can't
All my thoughts just bubble up inside me
Ready to explode
But they never do
That's worse
And they make it happen

   Them

I'm forced to bear the punches
I'm strictly made to bear the kicks
But what I really can't take is the ridicule
Sticks and stones will break my bones
But words will hurt me worse
And they do it

> *Them*

That's it, I'm done for
Someone saw and someone told
But I'll get the blame
Me, not her
Why me?
I'll run, I'll hide
But I'll never escape
Not those guys
Not

> *Them*

I'll have to face it
I'll have to do it sometime
Now
Sometime is now
I will walk up to the people
Who have put me in this state
I will walk

I am not afraid
I will do it without fear
Although I say that
I feel it
I feel it like it's taking over me
But I will win over it
Over

> *Them*

> *Them*

Their name echoes against my mind

> *Them*

It bangs against my ears

> *Them*

Although
I do not dare to let their names pass my cold lips

> *Them*

> *Them*

Bullies,   bullies

> *Them.*

Maya Owen (10)
Fairlop Primary School

The Busy Playground
(In the style of Bob Dylan)

I enter the busy playground,
Eating my healthy break,
Then I hear a funny sound,
I hear, 'For goodness sake',
The boys are muddy from playing football,
'What?' I hear one call,
As if he doesn't know.
Girls are sniggering loudly, so everyone can hear,
Gossiping near the fence,
Falling out with friends, trying to fake a tear,
Naughty children sent to the naughty bench,
Everyone's disappointed as the bell rings,
Teachers come to collect classes,
Tidying up all the play things,
Everybody looks glum as playtime passes.

April Podd (10)
Fingringhoe CE Primary School

Playground Time
(Inspired by Bob Dylan)

The purple waterfall was cracked,
The little ones said it was as deadly as a shark.

Gracefully the bluebells bloomed,
They were as sparkly as a starry night.

The stony, bumpy playground
Was so cramped it was like a dump.

The plants which were trampled on
Now were as lonely as a broken twig.

The red swings were crashed,
They were as abandoned as a 1,000-year-old alley.

The plants were as dead as Adolf Hitler,
They once were pink, now they are unhappy.

The big tree takes the sunshine away,
It is as dark as midnight.

The flowers fell off the wall, it was dreadful,
It was as sad as a funeral, seeing them mistreated.

Michaela Bartholomew (9)
Fingringhoe CE Primary School

The Playground Poem
(In the style of Bob Dylan)

I walked outside the classroom to get my unhealthy break
When I heard everyone screaming
Because they thought the skipping rope was a snake.
Bullies laughing as they held an infant child up high
And guess what? He was only up to one bully's thigh!
Friends arguing and falling out.
A little girl getting teased because her second name is Trout!
Boys cheering loudly because they'd scored.
Rubbish everywhere including apple cores.
The bin overflowing like a fountain.
Children playing on the step, pretending it's a mountain.
Others crying because they've fallen over.
Little boys playing with miniature Land Rovers.
Nerds sitting down and playing chess.
Who's gonna win? Is it Jess or Bess?
The school bell goes, everyone stands still
But there's always one person who doesn't, his name is Bill.
They all lined up, some still eating their break
And the skipping rope that looked like a snake
Was put away ready for the next break.
Then they all walked into the classroom and shut the door
And all that was left in the playground were the apple cores.

Aimee Salmon (10)
Fingringhoe CE Primary School

The Playground
(In the style of Bob Dylan)

Loud ringing bell sounded
As the children cheered
And ran out with joy
To their favourite place.

Funky and muddy
The playground
Smelt funny
Like a rotten egg.

Funny, muddy children
Play all day
Like little mad men.

Everybody laughed
At the poor boy
His poor, poor knee
As sore as a bruise on a peach.

A boy dropped his crisps
They got squashed by a lady
And he wept like a piggy on a farm.

Funky, groovy playground
Full of good and bad
A place full of memories
Everyone there is mad!

Sam Francis (11)
Fingringhoe CE Primary School

Bullies' Playground

The wide open playground was very hard
And two tiny children were running like a cheetah.

Tiny, mucky kids shouting like a roaring lion.

Grey teachers annoyed because of screaming scoundrels.

The children called the teachers 'stinky as a tramp!'
Tiny, titchy Tim was as lost as a blind bat.

Big bully Ben beat the little boy and the boy started to cry,
Then a teacher went and gave the bully a detention.

A grey child walked onto the mucky playground
And started to shriek at the teacher.

The teacher screamed because a big bully
Said her hair was grey with blue stripes.

A boy called Luke got bullied by Bill and Ben
But liked beating them up.

A nasty place, the playground.

Liam Clewley (11)
Fingringhoe CE Primary School

Skip, Hop, Jump
(In the style of Bob Dylan)

Crunchy, muddy leaves were shouting as loud as elephants
Very muddy children were running as clumsily as clowns
The concrete ground was sitting as deep as an ocean.

The playground is a noisy bus stop, children waiting until class
At half-past ten it is like the bus is nearly here,
But at ten to, it's time to go and everyone goes in.

The golden sun shining down like a yellow lollipop
Happy children, skipping, hopping, jumping
Sad, hurt children standing alone.

The playground is a huge kiddy pudding
Children being thrown in at half-past ten.

At half-past ten it is like they've all been mixed up,
But at ten to, it's time to go and everyone goes in.

Some are happy, some are sad now playtime is over,
The playground is as empty as a book with no words.

Rosina Turner (10)
Fingringhoe CE Primary School

Playground Poem
(In the style of Bob Dylan)

The tiny, happy children were playing in the playground,
When they heard a sound,
They were as happy as clowns.

It was a filthy brown puppy
And it was bounding towards them.

The filthy brown puppy had been rolling
In the dirty brown mud, then it ran away.

The boys were playing football
Then one of them scored a goal, then everyone cheered.

The girls were playing skipping with a little rhyme,
'Teddy bear, teddy bear turn around,
Teddy bear, teddy bear touch the ground.'

Playground is full of love and hate,
But everybody loves it.
It is great!

Philippa O'Toole (10)
Fingringhoe CE Primary School

Lion Cubs

Like silky lion cubs' fur
Clouds glitter and sparkle across winter skies
From cold and icy lands,
The lions' whiskers like trees' branches swaying in the breeze.
Icicles start to freeze in the cold snow
Just like lion cubs' fur
In the cold winter land it makes not a peep.

Sacha Jones (8)
Great Bardfield Primary School

Playful Children

Playful children
Unheated car
Dazzling ice
Frozen star

Pure snow
Screeching ice
As we go
In the speed of light

Nippy weather
Snowballs fly
Cold in winter
Jack Frost bites

Birds fly south
Menacing sky
Sit by fire
Warm up nice.

Joe Clark (9)
Great Bardfield Primary School

Winter Days

Snow glows
Skidding ice
Wind blows
Wrap up nice.

Blocked nose
Snow falls
Numb toes
Birds call.

Cup of tea
Take Ted
Warm up me
Go to bed.

Maggie Cooper (9)
Great Bardfield Primary School

Winter Days

Biting air
Winds blow
In the streets
Under snow

Ears red
Chilled breath
Cuddle Ted
At winter

Snow falls
Windows steamed
Slippery path
Dazzling stream

Snowy gutters
Hazardous lanes
Patterned frost
On windowpanes

Icy windows
Inclement night
Sparkly moon
Dazzling bright.

Dominic Baines (9)
Great Bardfield Primary School

Feathers

Snow falls like frozen feathers falling to the floor
Snow clouds like a peacock's wings fanned out
Peacocks show off their glistening feathers
Frozen peacocks spread over hills
Peacocks as still as rocks.

George Stephens (9)
Great Bardfield Primary School

Winter Days

Rushing air
Winds crash
Polar bears
In a dash.

Knees red
Runny nose
Rosy cheeks
Stiff toes.

Icy roads
Chimney smoke
Dripping drains
Cars raw.

Slushy gutters
Frosty patterns
On cold windows.

Marielle Dorset (8)
Great Bardfield Primary School

Winter

Glistening night,
Frosty streets,
Snowball fights
And some treats.

Insecure snow,
Skidding ice,
Moon glows,
No more life.

Church bells ring,
Christmas trees,
Children sing,
We are free.

Harris Churchman (8)
Great Bardfield Primary School

Winter Days

Snowball fights
Father and son
Cosy nights
Have lots of fun

Nippy snow
Never goes
Spirit of winter
Numb toes

Snowflakes fall
As fluffy as a feather
Sparkling in the night
As cold as the weather

Ice on road all around
Shimmering but lethal on the ground.
This poem will make you see
That winter's fun for you and me.

Ollie Bedding (10)
Great Bardfield Primary School

Winter Morning

I walked through the frosty fields
In the early morning dew.
Unique snowflakes falling, falling to the ground
And on the sparkling trees too.

I walked through a dark wood
And I heard the wind blow,
I slipped in an icy puddle
And fell into the cold snow.

A red nose and rosy cheeks,
With my woolly hat on my head,
That's the first thing I did,
When I got out of bed.

Natasha Jones (8)
Great Bardfield Primary School

Frosty Nightfalls

Lethal wind
A horrible sight
Wild clouds
A dark night.

Nasty smell
Inclement weather
Cracking lakes
White feather.

Icicle roofs
Frosty cars
A frozen village
Very far.

Platinum hills
Twinkling leaves
Dangerous roads
Silvery trees.

Time to awake
Get out of bed
Very cold
Frozen head.

Helena Terry (9)
Great Bardfield Primary School

The Sparrow

He flaps like a maniac across the rosy dawn,
He lifts his head once he's landed on his perch.
He starts to sing a high-pitched note,
Then flies again, this time he floats.

Georgina Bray (10)
Great Bardfield Primary School

Snowy Days

Snowy streets
Chilly airs
Snow as pure
As polar bears

Rosy noses
Shimmering lips
Threatening winds
Children doing flips

Amusing snowmen
On the roads
Shimmering rooftops
Icy stone toads

Sleet in gutters
Ice in drains
Twinkling stars
Sparkling lanes

Stretching time
Night has done
Get up now
Morn has won.

Laura Graham (9)
Great Bardfield Primary School

Icy Air

Nippy air
Frozen clouds
Polar bear
Hunting round

Noses red
Sore lips
Frozen ears
Lots of sips

Smoky chimneys
Cars skidding
Falling snow
On garden walls

Snow in gutters
Icebergs falling
Frozen patterns
On windows

Morning call
Wake up
Cold by snow
Sleep in bed.

Cam Meldrum (11)
Great Bardfield Primary School

Winter

Nippy air
Snowball fights
Streetlamps glow
In the night

A glossy sheet
All white
Shovelling snow
With all your might

Heating on
Icy lanes
Melted snow
Down the drains

Unpredictable patches
Laughter's there
Running on
Through the air

Snow is falling
Pristine look
Stay nice and warm
With a book.

Katie Rees (10)
Great Bardfield Primary School

Winter

Spotless fields
Nippy breeze
Blowing by
In the trees

Blinding light
In the sky
Not too hot
So snow won't dry

Perilous surfaces
Some may fall
Frozen moss
On the garden wall

The roadside pavement
Covered in sleet
Children laughing
In the street

Under the covers
Snuggle down
Nice and warm
In dressing gown.

Eleanor Jones (9)
Great Bardfield Primary School

Winter Days

Nippy breeze
air rushes
countryside
strong gushes.

Rosy cheeks
stiff ears
noses red
frozen tears.

Chimneys smoke
glossy weather
piled snow
wrapped in leather.

Icy lanes
chilly air
snow as pure
as polar bears.

Wake up now
rise and shine
all the snow
is mine all mine.

India Witham (10)
Great Bardfield Primary School

Cold Day

It's a cold day
Children playing in the snow
Flicking snowballs
Here we go.

Nippy weather
Breath smokes
People walking
But then they choke.

Slippy sleet
On the path
Car skidding
As people laugh.

Red noses
Frozen lip
Runny eyes
Creaky hips.

Stacey Gibson (10)
Great Bardfield Primary School

My Anger

My anger creeps up on me like a devil,
which turns me bright red.
That means danger is ahead.

My anger makes me violent,
I punch, kick and then I row.
Next, I bite, pinch and growl.

My anger starts inside me like a volcano,
when it erupts it makes me aggressive
like a bull.

Cameron Ayling (9)
Great Bradfords Junior School

My Feelings

My anger is there when my happiness hides inside me
When my happiness is there my anger waits patiently and peacefully
Until I get furious again.

My anger comes quickly like a horse galloping towards me
Knocking every person in its path
Showing no respect to anyone.

My anger spins quickly to me like a tornado
Catching and grabbing people in its way
Leaving no track of a single person or animal.

My happiness slithers to me like a snake
In the green and bright rainforest
Finding its family.

My happiness rises upon me like a sunrise
In the bright and early morning.

My happiness whispers to me
Like a breeze of air rustling the leaves of the trees.

My happiness shines like flames of fire.

Ji Young Lee (9)
Great Bradfords Junior School

Sunday Is My Day

Sunday is my day.

Lying on the sofa like I have been stunned,
watching cartoons.

Munching crisps so loud it shakes the whole house,
laughing like a hyena at the TV shows.

Resting like a sleeping dog
and snoring like a bulldozer.

Sunday is my day.

Rhys Kelly (9)
Great Bradfords Junior School

Mixed Emotions

My anger erupts with red lava inside me
Burning my happiness away
My happiness is consumed by the lava
While my anger laughs and laughs

My anger is like a fierce lion
Slowly stalking me
Getting ready to jump and charge
Taking me as its prey

My anger is like a tornado
Sucking up my happiness
Leaving me alone with anger
Till my happiness floats back to me.

My happiness never leaves me
Like a duckling following his mother
Sometimes hidden under her wing
From the shadows of fear

My happiness comforts me
Like a warm, comfy bed
But when my anger returns to me
It takes me to the dead

My happiness leaves me with surprises
Joy never-ending
But when I am having all this fun
Sometimes my anger creeps back.

Samuel Stedman (9)
Great Bradfords Junior School

Anger And Happiness

My anger attacks me
Like a bullet from a gun
Leaving no survivors in its path
Cold and hard

My anger blanks my mind of all that is good
Stealing all kinds of hope
When I get up it forces me back down
Making me angrier and angrier
Each time it knocks me down

My anger sits in front of me
Staring with its evil red eyes
Slowly invading my mind
Filling my brain with thoughts so devastating.

        My happiness overcomes my terrifying thoughts
        Taking them far away
        Without exception

        My happiness strikes me with a powerful blast
        Like a lightning bolt
        Making me laugh in pain
        Each time it hits me.

Matthew Horne (10)
Great Bradfords Junior School

My Love

My love is like roses on a summer's eve,
soft, gentle, so elegant it's hard to believe.

It's like holding a sweet smile in my hands,
so breathtaking, beautiful, it's so grand.

My love is like roses on a summer's eve,
soft, gentle, so elegant it's hard to believe.

Alexandra Jenkins (9)
Great Bradfords Junior School

My Feelings

My anger blackens everything like a shadow
Swallowing everybody's happiness as it passes them
Turning them black and angry

My anger is like a black bull
Charging at a red cloak
Bashing everything with anger as it passes

My anger boils up inside me
Like a volcano full of lava
About to erupt
Ready to burn everything in its path

                    Happiness lights up inside me
                    Like lightning in a midnight sky
                    Every part of me glowing

            My happiness freezes all of my bad thoughts
            Making them lifeless like an ice sculpture
            Frozen so they can't reach me

                My happiness fills me with surprises
                    A birthday every day
                A newborn baby into my family
                    A never-ending smile.

Dominick Wiseman (9)
Great Bradfords Junior School

My Happiness

My happiness comes to me like a big fat present,
all wrapped up in shiny colours for me.

My happiness comes to me like animals being born,
when they discover how to walk.

My happiness comes to me when my friends are happy
when I hear them laugh.

Larissa Clarke (10)
Great Bradfords Junior School

Mixed Emotions

My anger boils up inside me like a never-ending black hole
It feels like it's taking me far away
Telling me I am alone.

My anger waits for me like a bee
Ready to take me to its nest to sting
I go red
Like a violent volcano.

My anger comes to me like thunder
Making a dangerous sound
Deadly and ready to kill
Not knowing when to stop.

My happiness creeps up on me like a dolphin
With his shining skin glowing brightly in the sunrise
Rising in the distance
I follow him wherever he leads me.

My happiness sits in front of me like a quiet butterfly
Calm and beautiful
Silently whispering to me
Like the golden shore.

My happiness boils up inside me like an egg ready to hatch
The birds singing silently
Ready for the pretty birds to arrive.

Adam Pillinger (9)
Great Bradfords Junior School

My Anger

My anger explodes into a million bad memories in my mind
and destroys all happiness, love and all things calm in my mind.

My anger sucks me up like a wormhole
and spits me on a planet with only pain, death and sadness.

This anger of mine is so destructive
not even the power of a violent volcano can stop it.

Ryan Cheek (9)
Great Bradfords Junior School

Mixed Emotion

My anger comes to me like a big black thunder cloud
Filled with rain and coldness
Ready for the storm

My anger crawls up on me like a spider
Trying to catch a fly to wrap up in its web
Ready to eat

My anger comes to me when my sister freaks me out at night
When we are all asleep

My anger is in my head like a baby screaming
Loudly and clearly

My happiness comes to me when I see glittering snowflakes
Falling from the sky like diamonds on the ground
Shining brightly round

My happiness comes to me when I smell my mum's
Delicious roast dinner filling the air
My tummy starts to rumble as we run to the table

My happiness comes to me when I am snuggled up in my bed
Knowing that it is cold and chilly outside
And the stars are shining in the sky.

Carly Ellis (9)
Great Bradfords Junior School

Cats

When cats curl up,
they look like a pile of clothes.

When cats sit in front of you,
they can stare at you like a statue.

When cats sleep softly,
they are peaceful and quiet.

When cats purr quietly,
they are as sweet as sugar.

Lucy Norwood (10)
Great Bradfords Junior School

Fear

The hair on my neck stands up
I hear every single creak
My stomach is twirling and whirling
My eyes are looking around

My face goes white
I get goose pimples
I just can't help it
Oh no! The exam is here.

Jamie Copus (9)
Great Bradfords Junior School

My Anger

My anger makes me explode into a ball of fire,
flames burning through anything they can.

My anger makes me crack into pieces,
like glass shattering, beyond repair.

My anger destroys me like a storm force wind,
hitting me like a lashing, thundery rain.

It hurts me like a blow in the stomach.

Ellis Graham (10)
Great Bradfords Junior School

Anger Is

Anger sounds like people shouting,
Anger looks like a bull charging at you,
Anger smells like smelly socks,
Anger reminds me of rotten eggs,
Anger makes my blood run cold,
Anger makes me feel out of control,
Anger makes me think I'm going to blow!

Shaun Whiteley (10)
Great Bradfords Junior School

Chocolate

Chocolate can be hard,
but I also like it runny,
when I go and eat it,
I have to hide it from my mummy!

Because my mum's a chocolate monster,
she'd eat it night and day,
when she's eating chocolate,
remember, stay out of her way!

Well you see I'm just as bad,
I must get it from my mum,
I would eat it night and day,
from nightfall through to sun.

So all you people out there,
please stop and beware,
my mum and me with chocolate,
will never, never share.

Amie Blackburn (9)
Great Bradfords Junior School

My Anger

My anger smashes through every wall in every town.
It tastes like burnt crisps and looks like maggots.
It makes a flesh-crunching, ear-shattering sound.
My anger waits for me like a spitting cobra
Ready to poison me.

My knuckles dripping with streams of blood
As I
Scream
Out loud
My ears steam up.

My anger is like a lion ready to kill suddenly . . .
Aaah!

Darren Brown (9)
Great Bradfords Junior School

My Anger

My anger blows up inside me like a volcano,
filled with lava,
red and hot,
as hot as fire.

My anger prowls menacingly like a tiger,
pouncing on its prey,
ready to eat me,
fierce and brave.

My anger destroys me like fire,
burning with flames,
bright and orange.

My anger is like thunder,
making a loud, angry noise,
in the dark, angry sky.

Joanna Bray (9)
Great Bradfords Junior School

My Feelings

My happiness comforts me like a cuddly blanket
and talks to me when I am with my mum
and smells like a field of daffodils.

My sadness comes to me like a bolt of lightning
and is like the sound of a waterfall
crashing down on a summer's day.

My anger is like a volcano about to erupt,
when my friends and I break up
when I'm scared of the dark
when I'm all alone.

Rebecca Collar (9)
Great Bradfords Junior School

My Anger

My anger builds up inside me
like an earthquake
destroying everything in its path.

My anger blows inside me
like a hurricane, ripping everything to pieces.
It does not know how to stop.

My anger destroys me,
my fists are clenched tight, suddenly . . .
Argh! It gives me a massive fright.

Jedariah Noble-Hull (9)
Great Bradfords Junior School

My Anger

My anger waits for me like a volcano waiting to erupt,
red-hot fire flows through my veins,
like boiling lava out of a volcano.

When my anger starts I see red all over,
I am like a lion ready to pounce,
as hot as fire.

My anger sits in front of me,
like a black hole ready to suck me up.
No way out of this darkness,
it just keeps on going . . .

Alexander Newman (10)
Great Bradfords Junior School

The Castle On The Hill

On the hill, there is a castle.
Round the castle, there is a moat.
Over the moat, there is a bridge.
Beyond the bridge, there is a door.
Through the door, there is a courtyard.
Across the courtyard, there stands a tower.
Inside the tower, there is a staircase.
Up the staircase, there is a door.
Across the door, iron locks are bolted.
Behind the door, there lies a young girl,
Lying peacefully in her bed.
She awaits a young man to rescue her one day.
Then she will be free to love him.
She will be happy for all her days.

Abbie Green (9)
Great Bradfords Junior School

My Anger

My anger strikes like lightning, firing in the sky.
With no warning it hits me and takes over my body.

My anger boils up inside me like a violent volcano,
hot and ready to explode.
Steam spilling from my mouth.

My anger kills me like a fireball,
raging through a city,
destroying everything in its path,
leaving nothing but itself.

Maria Thomas (9)
Great Bradfords Junior School

My Happiness

My happiness is like a chain
It can never be broken by hand
Strong and thick.

My friends are like my happiness
Never leaving me
Always there
Never far away.

My happiness swirls around me
Protecting me from harm
Never stopping
Never ending.

My happiness calls to me
Like a seagull to the sea
Gently touching me.

Abbie Pillet (10)
Great Bradfords Junior School

My Anger

My anger is like red fireballs in the sun
burning out.

My anger is like an explosion,
creeping up to me as silent as a mouse.

My anger is as powerful as a dinosaur,
charging at the world.

My anger is like steam,
escaping from a whistling kettle.

My anger disappears as slow as a snail,
hiding away, waiting and ready to pounce again.

Ryan Sycamore (10)
Great Bradfords Junior School

My Anger

My anger boils up inside me like a fireball,
Exploding into a million pieces.

My anger prowls menacingly like a wolf,
Stalking its prey, crouching and ready to pounce.

My anger stalks like a tiger, tensely waiting for the kill.
My anger destroys me like a fire,
Raging across grass in the summer,
Savaging everything in its path.

My anger strikes like a bolt of lightning,
Silent, but with so much power,
Like the sun burning up inside me.

My anger disappears as quick as a flash,
Where it goes I do not know,
Resting like a lion waiting in silence.

William Stephens (9)
Great Bradfords Junior School

Happiness And Anger

My happiness comes to me
when a big smile grows on my friend's face.

My happiness comes to me
like a snake slithering through the wet green grass.

My happiness comes to me
when it's Christmas and I get lots of colourful presents.

My anger comes to me
like a raining cloud, when it's thunder and lightning.

My anger comes to me
when my friends have a fall out, it makes me sad.

My anger comes up to me
when someone dies in my family, it feels like it's all my fault.

Stephanie Turner (9)
Great Bradfords Junior School

Anger

Anger sounds like a boom and a crash to me,
Anger looks like a fire, redness in my eyes.
Anger smells like cigarette smoke going up my nose,
Anger tastes like dry, hard chalk, very bad.
Anger feels like a cobra gripping you with all its strength,
Anger reminds me of funerals
And going to the graveyard on Christmas Eve.
Anger, I think of blood and death and dying.

Rosie Irons (10)
Great Bradfords Junior School

Happiness Is

Happiness is laughing and playing and having a good time.
Happiness is a hot summer's day.
Happiness is snowball fights and building snowmen.
Happiness reminds me of mischief.
Happiness makes me smile and laugh.
Happiness makes my face shine up.
Happiness makes me explode with happiness!

Nathan Gypps (10)
Great Bradfords Junior School

Anger

Anger sounds like people shouting.
Anger looks like a volcano going to erupt.
Anger feels like a *big* explosion inside me.
Anger smells like rotten eggs.
Anger reminds me of a fire blazing straight into my eyes.
Anger tastes like blood streaming through my mouth.

Alex Miller (9)
Great Bradfords Junior School

Feel The Anger

Anger sounds like cars crashing,
I look around and see bashing.
It feels like my blood has run cold,
The next thing I know, I smell old.
Sometimes it makes me remember the bad times I've had
And now you know how anger feels.

Micah Salmon (9)
Great Bradfords Junior School

That Scare

I'm waiting.
I'm waiting for that scare.
I've got butterflies in my tummy.

I'm scared,
So scared.
My breathing's getting louder by the second,
My head is spinning around and around.

It's coming,
It's coming.
Then suddenly . . .
Help!

Sophie Bass (9)
Great Bradfords Junior School

Anger

Anger sounds like people getting a divorce,
Anger looks like people getting hurt,
Anger smells like a burning fire,
Anger feels like needles digging into my flesh,
Anger reminds me of adults fighting,
Anger is a bad memory.

Keren Pegg (10)
Great Bradfords Junior School

Humour To Me . . .

Humour to me is laughter and fun.
Humour to me is an iced bun.
Humour is Miss Loxley in a gym suit.
Humour is Mr Cosslett in a pink tutu.
Humour is Alex in the goal.
Humour is Shaun whacking the door.

Humour to me is fun and games.
Humour makes me feel happy.
Humour is Mr Moulton on the swing.
Humour is Miss O'Brien in the pool.
Humour is Megan driving a car.
Humour is Mrs Powell doing karate.
Humour is Rachel in a bunny outfit.
Humour is Adam getting hit with a custard pie.

Charlie Schofield (10)
Great Bradfords Junior School

My Anger

My anger is like a bomb ready to explode.
My anger creeps up on me like a gunshot.
My anger is like a dinosaur ready to roar.
My anger is like a volcano waiting to erupt.
My anger roars like a lion ready to kill.

My anger is a hurricane blowing down a building.
My anger is like someone has been shot.
My anger is like a shark ready to catch his prey.
My anger is like a helicopter bashing everything out of the way.

My anger is a tornado ripping everything into pieces,
But cannot stop.

Paul Saunders (9)
Great Bradfords Junior School

Funny

Funny tastes like mushy peas,
It makes my eyes water
And makes me crack up.

Funny smells like doughnuts
It makes me fall off chairs
And fall down stairs.

Funny sounds like lots of laughter,
It makes my sides split
And makes me hold my chest.

Funny is like a custard pie,
You are going to get it
In your face.

Adam Sharman (10)
Great Bradfords Junior School

Valentine's Day

Valentine's Day is on the way and love is in the air.
I've got to send valentine cards, but to who?
Oh it's just not fair!

Peter, Lewis, David or Paul, who should I choose?
Oh I don't know at all! If I only choose one, the others will get mad
And if I choose no one at all then I'll feel so bad.

But what about the gifts, there are too many sorts,
But wait, aren't they special just because of the thought?

Love is in the air is what people say,
Oh and remember a loved one is cherished always
Not just for Valentine's Day!

Megan Craig (10)
Great Bradfords Junior School

Me

My anger is red and black
Dark colours
Red is danger and black is a hole

My anger makes me shiver down my spine
Like a blizzard swirling around me
Horrible
Cold

My anger is a tiger and a lion
Roaring at me
Putting their claws into me
It's terrible

That's my anger.

Lucy Ogan (10)
Great Bradfords Junior School

Happiness

My happiness is the colour yellow like the sun
It tastes like sweet strawberries melting slowly in my mouth,
It is the smell of a candle flame dancing in the wind
And is a rainbow showing me God's promise.

Happiness is a smile, greeting me in the morning light
And happiness tickles me inside.
My happiness is a hug from my mum and dad
And is a tiny baby's first word.
Happiness is sitting around an open fire with your family
And is snow falling silently outside.

Bronwyn Morley (9)
Great Bradfords Junior School

Dear Sister

Dear Sister,
While you were out
Your computer went and broke itself on purpose,
Your CD player pushed itself out of the window,
Your hamster selfishly went and drowned itself in the bath,
Just to annoy me, your homework decided to spill my drink
                                                  all over itself.
I don't think we'll ever work out how the cat ruined your favourite dress.
I was downstairs all this time (honest).
So knowing you're going to blame me,
I've gone to Auntie Ellie's to, well, hide!

Nia Griffiths (10)
Great Bradfords Junior School

Humour

Funny is my dad breaking a pot
Trying to balance it on his head.
When it started to wobble, we all stomped.
The pot fell off and we laughed till our mouths were tired.

Funny smells like rotten eggs.
It makes me go mad.
It's a tomato getting squished.
Funny is a baby laughing
It makes me talk loudly,
Or am I just totally mad?

Ben Phillips (10)
Great Bradfords Junior School

Anger

Anger is somebody suffering
Anger is a fire burning
All across the trees
Anger is somebody suffering
Anger is cars smashing
Anger is angry bees
Anger is boiling lava
Anger is chasing seas
Anger smells like soles
Anger tastes like raw fruit sitting on a tree.

Zoe Soraf (9)
Great Bradfords Junior School

Anger

Anger sounds like an overloaded radio.
Anger looks like a volcano erupting.
Anger smells like sweaty gym socks.
Anger feels like you're about to bleed.
Anger reminds me of death and murder.
Anger's movement is pointing and pushing.
Anger tastes like Brussels sprouts.
Anger, I think of blood and fighting.

Kieran Notley (9)
Great Bradfords Junior School

Anger

Anger sounds like my brother crying.
Anger looks like a meteor crashing to the ground.
Anger smells like the ground burning.
Anger reminds me of my grandad's funeral.
Anger makes me think of nothing at all
Anger tastes like a piece of coal.
Anger is a bad memory.

Owen Hoare (10)
Great Bradfords Junior School

The Blitz

Darkness covers the whole of the town,
Some unfortunate people fall down,
The air raid siren sounds off,
Put on your gas masks or you may cough.

The shelters are as cold as winter ice,
The gas fills your lungs,
Stinging like a splinter,
Like propaganda made by Hitler.

The air raid siren is not yet all clear
And after an hour it hurts your ear.
The warden checks for any sign of light,
The bombers roaring at a great height.

Torches allow very little light,
The cover of the torch is very tight.

Fokker Wulfes travel at a speed
People drink smuggled mead.

The air raid siren is not yet all clear,
There's a sudden freeze, fear of death.
The spitfires race in
And the dogfight is about to begin.

Danny Christie (10)
Holland Park Primary School

World War Chaos

Big, bulldozing bombs crashing to the ground,
Extremely enormous explosions eating up people's lives,
Screeching, screaming sirens,
Flamingly furious fires, ferociously tearing down buildings.
Smelly, smoky streets,
Satisfyingly, speedy Spitfire gliding through the air.
Boom! The Spitfire's down.

Alex Cox (11)
Holland Park Primary School

The Stampede

A quiet village in Sri Lanka,
Lots of fun and lots of laughter,
But the sucking sea starts to bubble,
Such strange events can only mean trouble.

Like a stampede the tsunami comes
Running, roaring and raging,
Like a herd of elephants charging on their way
Like hungry tigers hunting their prey.

No longer golden beaches,
Now a terrible sight,
No more fun and laughter,
But frantic people running in fright.

Climbing onto rooftops,
They haven't got long,
The stampede is coming closer,
Two minutes later the village is gone.

No more fun and laughter,
No smile on any face,
One wave has caused,
Such a sad place.

Ava Pickett (11)
Holland Park Primary School

My Breakfast

Runny fried egg
Hot buttered toast
That's the meal
I love the most
I need a good breakfast
To power my brain
Or else my attention
Is bound to wane!

Nicky Fillingham (7)
Holland Park Primary School

Different Living

Children crying, mothers grieving,
Hearts broken, families scarred,
Ripped apart by the claws of the humungous wave,
Orphaned children left alone,
No family, no home,
Desperate parents searching the rubble,
No family, no home,
People starving,
Craving water they have not got,
Hundreds dying from deadly diseases,
Tetanus, cholera, typhoid.
Death!

Children laughing, mothers cooking,
Hearts happy, families together,
Drawn together by happiness and faith,
Joyful children playing all day long,
Happy families, comfortable homes,
Proud parents smiling at their offspring,
Happy families, comfortable homes,
People eating hearty meals,
Drinking fresh, cool water straight from the tap,
Hundreds cured from diseases,
Antibiotics, tablets, injections, *relief!*
How different life can be.

Georgia Hickey (10)
Holland Park Primary School

Davey My Uncle

I have a uncle called Davey,
Who works as a chef in the navy.
He cooks for the Queen,
On the food I am keen,
Apart from his lumpy old gravy.

Madeline Allis (8)
Holland Park Primary School

The Seasons

Spring is here,
The days are getting longer,
The fields are a rainbow of colour
And the birds are coming home.

Summer's here,
The beach is cooling,
Fun awaits in the blistering heat,
Can't wait until six weeks.

Autumn is here,
The leaves are falling,
I can't wait to jump around in the crunchy leaves.

Winter is here,
My birthday is soon,
I'm very lucky 'cause Christmas will follow
And the snow will make it even better.

Megan Steel (11)
Holland Park Primary School

The Wave Of Hell

Playing about
Having fun on the beach
The sea was calm
Not a cloud in the sky
Suddenly the wave of hell came
Deadly and dangerous
Destroying houses
Roaring, it ran, ruining lives
Bodies floating in rubble
No one playing about
No one having fun on the beach.

Hannah Munford (10)
Holland Park Primary School

The Christmas Tree

My job is not exciting
But it's good enough for me
If you look in your living room at Christmas
I am your Christmas tree.

All spiky and green
On the end of my branches there are baubles
I have an angel on top of me
And I do not wear goggles.

I have pretty tinsel around me
Which sometimes tickles my legs
Sometimes people put presents on me
Oh, by the way, the angel is called Megs.

When Christmas is over
The humans pack me away
But when Christmas comes again
I come out and say . . .
Merry Christmas everyone.

Bethany Godwin (9)
Holland Park Primary School

The Blitz

Empty streets,
Bloodstained walls,
Bombed houses,
Not a house standing.

Dead bodies,
Severed limbs,
Praying for help,
Ambulance sirens,
Bombs exploding,
Boom!
There's no one left.

Tyler Rendell (10)
Holland Park Primary School

Favourite Things

This is what I like to do
In my spare time after school!
I look after my pets Bash and Tav,
Bash is a hamster and Tav is a tortoise,
I feed them every morning and night,
Seed and cucumber suit them alright.
Reading books is also good fun,
Especially if it's a horror one,
Cooking also interests me,
When I bake cakes for tea.
Playing out, making dens,
In the gardens with my friends.
We also like to ride our bikes,
Thrashing through the mud and pulling stunts.
Chilling out on a Sunday afternoon
Before I'm told to clean my room!

Liam Torr-Clark (10)
Holland Park Primary School

Blitz

Hear the sirens go again,
Planes and bombs have come to fight,
Hear them come over our own house
Dropping bombs with all their might!

Mum rushes us to the shelter
A bomb goes off in the street
Mum cuddles my sister
Someone really must have died!

As we hear a rattle, all our gas masks go on.
I want to scream,
A doodlebug flies over,
Then it stops, this won't be long.

Screams and shouts from next door.
Did it drop? We can't be sure.

Jasmine Swinbourne (11)
Holland Park Primary School

Brazilian Wonders!

Brazil, Brazil the country of delight.
Different people - black meets white.

Carnivals are an honour to view.
Why don't you come along too?

Colours and patterns displayed on the float.
Samba dances rocking the boat.

Brazil, Brazil the country of delight.
Different people - black meets white.

The rainforests have many features
As well as their fantastic creatures.

Monkeys and toucans - the birds fly so high
Frequent rain comes from the sky.

Brazil, Brazil the country of delight.
Different people - black meets white.

Like a crystal that shimmers.
There in clear waters.

Jasmine Allen (11)
Holland Park Primary School

Netball Poem

Netball, netball is the best,
Better than all the rest,
Holland Park are a great team,
But some are really mean.

It's a sport for anyone,
But just make sure you're fit to run,
You can come and join in the club,
It's better than going down the pub.

Get on your trainers and go out there,
But just make sure you don't stop and stare,
So come on out, we will welcome you,
We'll make sure it's nice to do.

Katie Herbert (10)
Holland Park Primary School

Gremlins

Gremlins . . .
They steal your jaffa cakes,
My mum's garden rakes
And drink your milkshakes.

My dad's car keys,
A wedge of cheese,
Well at least they took the mushy peas!

Toilet roll when you need it most;
That slice of lovely beans on toast.

My pocket money
Now that's not funny.
A tissue for when your nose is runny.

The cream for a blister,
The mat when you're playing Twister,
Oh dear,
I do apologise to gremlins everywhere.
It was my older sister!

Bradley R Hackett (11)
Holland Park Primary School

Tsunami - Death And Destruction

Death and destruction hit the beaches,
as the tsunami wave roared in that day,
racing as fast as a pack of cheetahs
pouncing on their prey.

Houses blown to smithereens,
walls and ceilings smashed,
hotels collapsed like a pack of cards,
leaving a carpet of muck and rubble.

'Where's my mum?' you hear them cry,
but their mothers have passed by,
their lives were washed away,
by the ferocious waves on Boxing Day.

Christopher Gadeke (11)
Holland Park Primary School

Wave Of Destruction

The deadly wave came,
People knocked off their feet,
Swept away,
Never to be seen again.

Houses destroyed,
Trees uprooted,
No one's safe,
Babies crying,
Children dying,
No one's safe,
Mums searching,
Dads rushing,
No one's safe.

The wave's gone,
Returned to the ocean,
From the shore,
Leaving a trail of
Devastated towns,
Millions *Dead!*
Mourning families,
Praying.

No one was safe
When the deadly wave came.

Gemma Gardiner (10)
Holland Park Primary School

Come On England

'Come on England!' was the roar,
It looked like England were about to score,
The ball was driven along the floor,
Once again there was a roar,
But this time David Beckham did score
Unlike before,
'Come on England!' was the roar.

Max Gage (10)
Holland Park Primary School

Run For Shelter

Streets emptied,
No houses at all,
Bombs exploding,
Babies sobbing,
Dark shelters,
Siren sounding,
Run, run.

People freezing,
Pitch-black,
Mums worrying,
Dads scurrying,
Suddenly . . .
Boom! Boom!
Pain, hurting,
Everything over.

Matthew Illsley (10)
Holland Park Primary School

Wave Of Destruction

Christmas Day over,
Boxing Day is here,
A killer wave approaches
And the beach is cleared.

Parents swept away,
Children alone,
Babies drowned,
How many lives gone?

Villages struck,
Houses trashed,
Left only rubble and muck,
Everything is smashed.

Chloe Nicholson (11)
Holland Park Primary School

Autumn Days

Big bonfire
Sparklers bright
Frozen toes
Chill, dark night.

Blue lips
Frozen toes
Nice hot soup
Round Uncle Joe's!

Megan Larkins (8)
Holland Park Primary School

Summer Days

Have a picnic
Swim in the sea
Cream bun
Home for tea

Play a game
Have some fun
Thick, sticky sand
Home with Mum!

Paige Dawson (8)
Holland Park Primary School

Playtime

P eople play with each other,
L ots of kids play with skipping ropes
A nd children fall over and get hurt,
Y ou better play safely.
T ell us what games you play,
I n the lunchtime break,
M y friends are really nice,
E very child has *fun!*

Nancy Sword (8)
Holland Park Primary School

A Flood Of Tears

A flood of waves,
A flood of tears,
A day of death,
A day of fears.

The sun was shining,
The sun was bright,
Then came the water,
Then came the fright.

Christmas Day over,
Boxing Day morning,
Death hit the beaches,
Boxing Day mourning.

Cling on for life,
Grab someone's arm,
Many swept to their death,
A few safe from harm.

Many parents gone,
Many children alone,
Where will they grow up?
What will they call home?

Aid is sent in,
Bought by navy and army,
Helping survivors
Of the Asian tsunami.

Isabella Roberts (10)
Holland Park Primary School

Oogle-Eye, Boogle-Eye

Oogle-eye, boogle-eye
What can you see?
A huge, blue dragonfly
Flying around me.

Oogle-eye, boogle-eye
What can you hear?
A gigantic black dog
Giving me fear.

Oogle-eye, boogle-eye
What can you smell?
Italian pizza
That tastes swell.

Oogle-eye, boogle-eye
What can you taste?
What's in my lunchbox?
Yucky fish paste.

Oogle-eye, boogle-eye
What can you feel?
A lovely blue dolphin
And an electric eel.

Millie Adler (8)
Holland Park Primary School

Summer Days

Have a picnic
Swim in the sea
Fizzy Coke
And a cup of tea.

Play a game
Have some fun
Bath towel out
Golden sun.

Amber Will (8)
Holland Park Primary School

My Day

I woke up this morning
And stopped snoring
Then I got dressed,
My dad was so stressed.

I'm at school
In the hall,
I sit down in my class
I watch people go past.

I'm eating lunch
My apple went crunch,
I'm out at play
Like on a normal day.

My subjects at school
Are so cool,
I do my homework at home
For some reason school won't leave me alone.

I have my dinner
I played a game, I was the winner
I read in my head
Then went to bed.

Holly Childerley (9)
Holland Park Primary School

The Playtime Poem

I play in the playground
All lunchtime,
With balls and skipping ropes
All lunchtime,
We have fun!

There is a really nice garden,
Behind the fence,
Full of flowers and garden butterflies,
But you have to jump, jump, jump.

Toms George (9)
Holland Park Primary School

Run For Shelter

'Run! Run! Run! for shelter
Save yourself my lad
Let all the bombs fall on me
Let me die in peace.'

Down the stairs
Along the hall
Into the Anderson shelter all.

Hear people crying
See people dying
Watch as your home falls down.

'Run! Run! Run! for shelter
Save yourself my lad
Drop all the bombs on me
Let me die in peace my lad
Save yourself, not me.'

Ryan Day (10)
Holland Park Primary School

My Family

My dad has a guitar
And the best car,
He's the best dad by far,
And makes me laugh ha-ha!

My mum cooks fabulous food,
When she's in the mood,
She fits in my heart,
Just like treacle tart.

My brother is a super star
And he likes to play with a toy car,
Sometimes he's a pain in the . . .
And always tells on me to Mum.

Hannah Harvey (9)
Holland Park Primary School

Horrible History

When you're sitting in history class,
So bored, not knowing what to do,
Just think of this poem,
It will see the hour through.

First there were the dangerous dinosaurs,
Tall, man-eating, with terrifying claws.
Then there was the early man,
Even older than your gran!

The Egyptians came next,
They invented hieroglyphics, their own text,
After that the Greeks had their reign,
And held the Olympic games.

Fighting Romans were the next craze,
Boy, did they have their special ways,
Then the Celts made their way in,
But unfortunately the Vikings took the win.

South American Incas were next in line,
But the Aztecs were in, in no time,
A few years later, medieval people had the power,
Their taste though, was rather sour.

The terrific Tudors were next to the stand,
The mighty rulers of all the land.
Prince Babur was rather a young king,
Only 14 when he took to that thing.

Then there was the American Civil War,
To stop slavery that's what they were fighting for,
After that there was Queen Vic,
The longest reigning monarch - what a trick.

Then broke out the First World War,
An awful sight - but there was more,
Hitler and his gang,
Had rather a big plan.

That will bring us to present day,
Hope you have enjoyed your class,
If you ever have a history test,
Then think of this poem and you will pass!

Ellen Gage (11)
Holland Park Primary School

When I Tasted . . .

When I tasted lettuce for the very first time
I sprinkled it with butter and herbs such as thyme!

When I tasted cabbage for the very first time
I said, 'Oh what a yucky taste,'
And Dad said, 'Oi, that's mine!'

When I tasted hamburger for the very first time
I poured tomato ketchup all over Mum's top!

When I tasted chips for the very first time
I puddled them in vinegar and made myself cry!

Charley Manners (10)
Holland Park Primary School

Playground

Playing in the playground,
Rushing here and there,
Playing with my friends,
Here, there and everywhere.

When I am playing chase,
It brings a smile to my face,
Running around having fun,
Underneath the summer sun.

Brea Blundell (9)
Holland Park Primary School

The Demon From Hell

He walks through Hell,
He leaves a trail of blood behind him,
His scales are as red as blood,
His teeth are as yellow as the sun,
His nails are as black as night,
His eyes are as blue as the sea.
He walks through mounds of rotting bones
As white as the moon,
He passes flesh-eating zombies
With skin as green as grass.
He passes pools of blood
With heaps of dead bodies surrounding them.
He enters the world of the living
Dropping corpses on the floor,
The people that see him live no more,
He eats people's souls, no mortal can ever harm him,
He terrorises humans. He takes them to Hell
Leaving a trail of blood wherever he goes,
He destroys buildings, he obliterates whole countries
Leaving the world like his home,
A living Hell!

Ryan Croke (10)
Holland Park Primary School

The Sky

The stars that sparkle in the sky
The Earth revolving day and night
The sun that shines
And makes day bright
The moon that glows
All the night
Saturn, Jupiter and shooting stars
Even a planet called Mars
(Sounds like a chocolate bar!)

Christopher Ashdown (11)
Holland Park Primary School

My Baby

Quick a tsunami!
It's heading for the beach,
Rush to my feet,
Where's my baby?
The waves still coming,
There's my baby,
Running towards him,
Scooping him up,
I'm being swept away,
Clinging to my baby.

Struggle for breath,
Holding my baby above the water,
See a tree,
Climbing to the top,
Cuddling my baby,
See a roof,
Have to jump.
Yes, I made it,
I am safe,
My baby is safe,
We are safe.

Gemma Day (10)
Holland Park Primary School

Dad

He is a tall tower,
He is a happy sun,
He is a sweet lollipop,
He is a cunning fox,
He is a gently flowing river,
He is a hilarious hamster,
He is a daddy-long-legs,
He is a light feather,
But most importantly he is my dad.

Gaby Baldock (11)
Holland Park Primary School

WWII

As the bombs fell to the floor,
Some of the people lived no more,
In the path of death and destruction,
Some of the men ceased to function,
'Run for shelter!' we heard them cry,
But were devastated when we saw they died,
And as I speak of this today,
I remember those who died on D-Day.

David Sayer (11)
Holland Park Primary School

School

School is fun
That's why we come

We come to learn
So we get an education to learn.

We come to school to see our mates
When something special is coming
We have a fête.

Grace Barlow (10)
Holland Park Primary School

The Teddy Bear And The Crocodile

There was a big crocodile,
Who had big beady eyes.
There was a little teddy bear,
Who was always telling lies!

He went snooping around,
Until he found a surprise.
There lay a crocodile,
He had never won a prize!

Kirsty Muir
Holland Park Primary School

The Wave Struck

Christmas has passed
Boxing Day is here
Wave comes surging over
Some people are no longer.

Parents have gone
Children left alone
Will they ever get a home?
The answer is nobody knows.

Villages crushed
Houses destroyed
Streets full of rubble
People full of fear.

Babies crying
Adults dying
Scary noises
Screaming and shouting from rooftops.

Chelsea Hindley (10)
Holland Park Primary School

Spring

Spring is on its way
And with it shall bring
The sweet smell of daisies and daffodils
Followed by blossom on the trees
Woken by the singing of the birds
And humming of the bees.

Spring is on its way
And with it shall bring
The sound of children
Playing in the spring breeze
Followed by the sun
Gleaming on the shimmering shore.

Amber Watts (10)
Holland Park Primary School

My Fruit Salad

Into the sundae glass
Go pieces of delicious strawberries,
Slices of screaming blackberries,
Drops of luscious kiwi fruit,
Chunks of mouth-watering melon,
Pieces of tempting, tropical pineapple,
Creamy, smooth bananas
And soft and round, tender grapes
Bursting with flavour
Pieces of scrumptious satsumas,
My tropical fruit salad, yum!

Rebecca Hoffman (11)
Holland Park Primary School

The Game

I get passed the ball,
I run down the wing,
All the crowd begin to sing,
I'm in the box,
A player to my left
And a player to my right,
I cross it in,
It hits my player on the head
And the next time I see him
He's in a hospital bed.

Tom Childerley (11)
Holland Park Primary School

My Birthday

My birthday is the best time of the year,
Woken up by birthday greetings,
Cards and presents to tear open,
What a surprise!
Everything I hoped for,
But here my mum comes with the birthday cake,
My family sings such a din,
Then we all go out for my birthday treat,
I have a most wonderful curry!
All too soon my day comes to an end,
Only 364 days recounting!

Kyle Lowis (11)
Holland Park Primary School

My Imaginary Cat

My cat is quick,
It likes to lick,
It's very furry
And a little bit hairy.
It's black and white,
Always ready to fight
And starts to jump,
He always likes a cheerful thump.
It's ready to pounce
And wants a bounce,
As it happily runs about.

Emily Hills (9)
Holland Park Primary School

Baby 81

Baby '81', an orphan
All alone
Baby '81' must be mine
I lost my baby to the wave
Baby '81' needs a mother
I need a son
I do hope baby '81' is mine
I will love him forever and ever
I will give him hugs and kisses
Baby '81' must be mine
I will fight for him
I will not give in
I must have baby '81'
Please!

Lydia Waller (10)
Holland Park Primary School

If I Could Paint A Picture . . .

If I could paint a picture
It would be of the sun going down,
The buildings would be glowing
All around the town.

If I could paint a picture
It would be of the moon and stars,
The buildings would have light on
And so would all the cars.

If I could paint a picture
It would be of children all asleep,
The buildings would be dark
As the children are asleep.

James Bettis (11)
Holland Park Primary School

My Old Teddy

I love you though your fur is worn out.
I love you though your arms are grubby and grey.
I love you though your ears are torn.
I love you though your paws are old.
I love you though your eyes are shabby and grey.
I love you though your tummy is flat.
I love you though the bow round your neck is ancient and floppy.
I love you, yes I love you teddy of mine.

Ami Fosker (8)
Holland Park Primary School

My World

When I'm in my own little world
I don't see the cruel, harsh outside world.
When my imagination runs away
I'm not nobody, I'm somebody.
When I'm on my own there's no one
To remind me of the reality of the world.
The mind is kind, you can be who you want to be,
Where you want to be, whenever you want.

Clare Gravatt (10)
Holland Park Primary School

Tsunami

T sunami was a terrible disaster, that struck on Boxing Day.
S hockwaves tore apart many families.
U nfortunately hundreds of thousands lost their lives.
N ow it's time for the whole world to reunite.
A mbulances rushed to their rescue, as the sea calmly drifted away.
M emories are sad of that heartbroken day.
I hope the world carries on raising money to help them rebuild
                              what the tsunami has taken away.

Charlotte Batchelor (10)
Holland Park Primary School

Me

My mum says she loves me
And so does my dad.
They always forgive me,
Even if I'm bad.
I'm not always happy
Sometimes I'm sad.
My brother and sister
Make me really, really mad.

I love my nan and grandad
And my pet cat Sabrina too
And without all my family
I would not know what to do.
I'm caring and I'm kind
And very bubbly too,
I just have my off day
Which everyone has too.

So really I'm not perfect
But then I'm only young,
So you'll have to excuse me
For I just like to have fun.

Loren Janes (10)
Holland Park Primary School

The Horse Poem

There was a horse called Sally
Who rode across the valley
She jumped over a hedge
And sat on the edge
Of a fast flowing river
And then began to snigger
Along came a horse called Tigger
Who happened to be a lot bigger
They played in the field
And a friendship was sealed.

Katherine Langdon (11)
Holland Park Primary School

The Sound Collector

(Based on 'The Sound Collector' by Roger McGough)

'A stranger called this morning
Dressed all in black and grey
Put every sound into a bag
And carried them away'

The blowing through the window
The clanging on the bed
The tapping on the table
And the banging in the shed

The sizzling of the saucepan
The squeak upon the chair
The rattling of the money
The buzz from my dad's lair

The snoring of the dog
And the noise of the TV
The screaming of our mums
And the laugh from you and me

'A stranger called this morning
He didn't leave his name
Left us only in silence
Life will never be the same'.

Anya Klarner (10)
Holland Park Primary School

Big Wave

The great big wave came,
The wave hit the beaches of Asia.
The cars crashed,
The boats were smashed,
The ants ran up the hill.
Some people dashed to high ground,
Some people died,
Some people survived,
The day the great big wave hit the beaches of Asia.

Ieuan Gledhill (10)
Holland Park Primary School

Tsunami Disaster

People lose their lives,
Tears streaming down their face.
All they can do is cry,
What happened to this place?

Water is everywhere,
Buildings tumbling to the ground.
People stand and stare,
Heartache is all around.

Money being raised,
Help is all around.
Everyone amazed,
Love and support is being found.

Clear up all the mess,
Rebuilding the shattered past.
Relieve a lot of stress,
There will be happiness at last.

Amy Wright (11)
Holland Park Primary School

Jump For Life

Here comes the killer wave
Bubbling onto the shore
The children are playing
The ladies are screaming
The men are sailing
Climbing into the palm trees
Sharks waiting to eat
People waiting to be rescued
Fighting for their lives
Praying for food and water.

Samantha Pinches (11)
Holland Park Primary School

The Sound Collector
(Based on 'The Sound Collector' by Roger McGough)

A stranger called this morning
Dressed in red and black
Put every sound into a bag
And carried them away

The buzzing of the microwave
The snoring of my dad
The rumbling of the car
The whistling of the wind

The beeping of the oven saying
My cakes are ready to eat
Hearing my mum reading to the baby
As she quietly falls asleep

*'A stranger called this morning
He didn't leave his name
He left us only silence
Life will never be the same'.*

Shannan Weeks (10)
Holland Park Primary School

Tsunami

26th December, a killer wave struck,
Hotels and villages left covered in muck,
Terrified people running to higher ground,
Adults and children crying, what a very sad sound.

Some fishermen lost, their boats broken in bits,
Homes and schools just piles of bricks,
Families left weeping, some now alone,
No clean food or water not even a home.

Non-uniform days and sponsored events,
Sending out money which will be well spent.

Sarah Watson (10)
Holland Park Primary School

A Recipe For My Munchy, Crunchy Mouth-Watering Fruit Salad

In my sundae glass I put . . .
Slivers of munchy, crunchy kiwi fruit,
Slices of succulent watermelon,
Sweet and sour-tasting pineapple
And creamy, juicy honeydew melon.

To make my munchy, crunchy, mouth-watering fruit salad
In my sundae glass I put segments of juicy mangoes,
Pieces of crunchy apple, chunks of delicious pear
And luscious lemon juice
To make my munchy, crunchy, mouth-watering fruit salad.

Harry Ryan (10)
Holland Park Primary School

Killer Wave

Sun-kissed beaches lie safe from harm,
Toddlers running into the lovely blue sea,
Many sunbathe with smiles on their faces,
No work to be done, time to relax.

Terrifying screams come from the beaches,
Houses knocked over like matchsticks,
The killer wave takes everything in its path,
People clinging onto palm trees, nobody is safe.

Piles of debris, scattered all over the ground,
Dead bodies, lying by the shore,
Millions starving, thousands diseased,
So many families torn apart by the killer wave.

Tom Wilkinson (10)
Holland Park Primary School

The Magic Box
(Based on 'Magic Box' by Kit Wright)

I will put in my box . . .
The first time I stood up and fell over,
The time I had my first cake and got it all over me,
The feel of my guinea pig's softness when she cuddled up to me.

I will put in my box . . .
The feel of my family's rabbit breathing,
The kindness of our cats purring gently on the couch,
The feel of my dog's licks on my face.

I will put in my box . . .
Lots of pencils and paper to write with,
Lots of art and craft glue to make lovely pictures,
Some love and care to keep us company.

Robyn Clemenson (8)
Holland Park Primary School

The Magic Box
(Based on 'Magic Box' by Kit Wright)

I will put in my box . . .
My favourite jack-in-the-box bouncing up and down
With a great big smile on his massive face
The noise of children crying and screaming.

I will put in my box . . .
My uncle's laugh
My special cat purring on my lap
The smell of my favourite breakfast.

I will put in my box . . .
My dog barking madly at birds
My friends laughing in the playground
The noise of the crowd cheering for Man U.

Mikey Irving (8)
Holland Park Primary School

The Magic Box
(Based on 'Magic Box' by Kit Wright)

I will put in my box . . .
The sweet smell of my great granny's sweet peas,
The fun memories of my past life,
The warm feel of all my cuddly teddies.

I will put in my box . . .
The first time I started to walk,
My ½ pence pieces that I was given when I was a baby,
My silver, shiny locket.

I will put in my box . . .
My special teddy I was given when I was a baby,
The warm feel of the fire,
The snug, warm feel when I'm in bed.

Rachel Clark (8)
Holland Park Primary School

Hogwarts

Hogwarts is a magic place,
Harry is ready to solve the case,
With villains like Voldemort there's no mistake,
If I were at Hogwarts I'd lie wide awake.

When the Dementors were there
A cold chill grew in the air,
In the grounds where the lake does lie,
Is where Sirius Black will soon die.

Sirius Black is captured and taken to the towers,
Hermione time travels and uses her powers,
They fly on Buckbeak through the air,
Said Sirius to Harry, 'We will soon be there.'

Georgia Humphries (9)
Holland Park Primary School

My Juicy Fruit Salad

Into my sundae glass
Go slices of juicy, crisp apple
Banana, soft and creamy
Big, sharp orange segments
Grapes, purple and plump
Strawberries, sweet and succulent
Plums, soft and tasty
Come and eat me!

Gabrielle Shaw (11)
Holland Park Primary School

My Cat Pepsi

My black cat is so fat
Through eating rats,
He's small and fluffy
And sneaks about.
Big blue eyes that stare at you,
He loves his running,
He leaps and jumps.
When it's time to go to bed
He snuggles up his little head.

Robyn Wiggins (9)
Holland Park Primary School

Autumn Days

Brown soup
Orange scarf
Children playing
What a laugh

Juicy burger
Hot dog
Burning fire
Burnt log.

Sean Hobbins (8)
Holland Park Primary School

What Is Pink?
(Based on 'What is Pink?' by Christina Rossetti)

What is pink? Babies are pink,
But sometimes babies also stink.
What is red? Blood is red,
Rolling down the small boy's leg.
What is blue? A box can be blue,
To carefully carry a brand new shoe.
What is white? Pansies are white,
Always pretty and full of light.
What is yellow? A sunflower is yellow,
Until they die, poor old fellows.
What is green? Cheese can be green,
But only if it isn't clean.
What is grey? Suits are grey,
Is someone wearing one today?
What is black? Cats are black,
Out at night, sniffing in a sack.

Bradley Reeve (8)
Holland Park Primary School

Tsunami

It started as just another day
As sun bright and glowing made us feel glad,
This was very soon to change making us feel very sad.
For far below the sea, the land was moving,
Unknown to us the sea would be rising.
It caught us unaware and most of us could only stare.
As the waves rolled towards us, growing bigger and bigger,
People started running quicker and quicker.
Which way to go to get away,
As high as you can, you must get away
That was what the people did say.
As the wave rolled away the shock and horror we saw.
Many people who stood there were gone
And would come back no more.

Sasha Leatherbarrow (10)
Holland Park Primary School

The Colour Collector
(Inspired by 'The Sound Collector' by Roger McGough)

'A stranger called this morning
Dressed all in black and grey
Put every colour into a bag
And carried them away'

The goldenness of cornflakes
The ivory of milk
The silverness of soup spoons
The see-throughness of silk

The greenness of tennis courts
When play has just begun
The orangeness of oranges
Glowing in the sun

The blueness of a dolphin
Nosing through the sea
The redness of a robin
Breasting in the tree

The creaminess of a polar bear
Sliding on the floes
The little piggy pinkness
Of tiny, tickly toes

The sky that smiled a rainbow
Now wears a leaden frown
Who's sobbing in his cavern
Wizzo the monochrome clown

'A stranger called this morning
He didn't leave his name
We live now in the shadows
Life will never be the same'.

Terry Baker (9)
Holland Park Primary School

My Secret Box
(Based on 'Magic Box' by Kit Wright)

I will put in my box . . .
The hoppity-skip of a bunny at play,
Opening the door to a warm summer's day,
Playing 'pretend' and 'follow the leader',
Topping up nuts in the winter bird feeder.

I will put in my box . . .
The tingling feeling I get
When I take my bunny to the vet,
Feeling happy, feeling sad,
Lying on the sofa hugging my mum and dad.

I will put in my box . . .
All of my toys,
But get rid of the stink of *smelly, old boys,*
My favourite friend (my old teddy bear),
My favourite trousers (my so-in flares).

I will put in my box . . .
The sun, the sky,
The animals, the world and my pet firefly.
My box is almost full now, I must stop.
But there's something else, and it's not a flashy top,
But peace and kindness and of course love,
And there's one last thing, a small, pure white dove.

Amelia Jardine
Holy Family RC Primary School

My Mum

My mum is the best
Because she cares for me
Looks after me
And makes dinner for me.

Thomas Kemp (9)
Mayflower Primary School

Tropical Forest

Well I'll tell you what I saw
Cos I saw just this.
There were lots of different colours,
And loads of rare shapes.
Shapes and sizes like
Circle and square,
And colours like
Orange and black
And pink and green.

Well I'll tell you what I heard
Cos I heard just this.
There was loads of noise like loud *roars,*
And leaves rustling.

Well I'll tell you what I felt
Cos I felt just this.
I felt amazed and surprised,
It was a big thrill.
Well I'll tell you something,
I'm coming here again.

Rebecca Lauder (10)
Mayflower Primary School

The Football Match

The football splashed onto the mud,
When the ball went in the net,
There was a girl with bruises and blood,
As she went down with a great big thud.

Then the crowd started to roar,
As we were trying hard to score,
But we didn't score a goal,
But we still all stood tall.

Lucy Young (10)
Mayflower Primary School

I Have A Friend

I have a friend
And he is great
But he has gone to war
On a field that looks like a crate.

I can hear screaming
And I can hear a shout
And I can see soldiers
Running through like a scout.

I feel scared
And I feel sad
I don't know where my friend is
And I feel rather bad.

Now the war is over
I can see the gore
And I can also see my friend
But I have him no more.

Erin Carman (9)
Mayflower Primary School

Tiger Tropical

Orange and black stripes passing by,
Claws like daggers, stabbing and scraping,
Trying to disguise behind leaves,
It's ready to strike at someone near,
Feeling nervous, ready to kill,
No one is safe at all.
Blood and guts going up the trees,
As the body lies on the floor, *dead!*
Petrified tiger walked away,
Feeling very guilty - walking home.

Amy Farrington (11)
Mayflower Primary School

The Greeks' Quest

Daringly, the Greeks were stabbing the hearts and souls,
The Trojans were fighting like mighty trolls,
Tactically, the Greeks got in a wooden horse,
The Trojans thought they won of course.

Happily, they celebrated all day,
The Trojans took in the horse,
The Greeks thought it was time to pay,
Powerfully, the Trojans used all their force.

The Greeks got out of the wooden block,
Suddenly the time was 7 o'clock,
The Trojans fell into a deep sleep,
Cunningly, the Greeks were ready to creep.

The Greeks were stabbing and striking,
Slowly the Trojans were dying,
Some white men were hiking,
That's the end of the fighting.

James Macdonald (10)
Mayflower Primary School

Shapes

A shape is amazing
All are amazing
The shapes are the best
Nothing is better.

I like a circle
It's better than ever
Nothing can beat it
Because it's the best shape.

My favourite shape
Is so great
I like this shape
Because it makes me shake.

Jordan Heath (10)
Mayflower Primary School

Tsunami

Oh why, oh why you ferocious beast
Cover all which was desirable?

You have broken hearts, homes, families and friends,
Why, oh why, oh why?

Suffering continues,
Blank hearts,
No more hopes,
Empty minds,
Diseases have spread,
Oh why, oh why?

You sicken me by what you have done,
Many people are dead and gone.
Oh why, oh why you monster of water,
Create a disaster where it is not needed?
Oh why, oh why?

Alex Chapman (11)
Mayflower Primary School

A Snow Tiger In A Snow Storm

Staggering in the blizzard, comes the snow-like tiger,
His fur is as white as frosted rings,
His eyes are sapphires glowing brightly,
His coat is as soft as a panda's fur.

The blizzard was getting worse, although he could smell something,
It was the radiant bird in the wood,
The bird was sitting on a branch,
It was feeding its young with insects.

The tiger shook his mighty paw on the tree,
The birds flew away, leaving her young,
The tiger tried to reach his dinner,
He carried the nest back to his home.

Bethany Starkings (10)
Mayflower Primary School

Maths

Fractions, fractions, ever so hard
No one gets them, no one gets them
People struggle, people struggle
Horrible things, horrible things

Addition, addition, easy, easy
People get it, people get it
Add two numbers, add two numbers
Easy subject, easy subject

Angles, angles, hard subject
Use a protractor, use a protractor
Hard to do, hard to do, hard to do
Worst subject, worst subject, worst subject

Shapes, shapes, triangles, triangles
Circles, circles, squares, squares
Very easy, very easy, very easy
Great subject, great subject

Decimals, decimals, quite hard
Some people get them, some people don't
Not a whole number, not a whole number
Like a fraction, like a fraction

Multiplication, multiplication
My favourite thing, my favourite thing
Times two numbers, times two numbers
Cool subject, cool subject

Division, division, hard, hard
Complicated, complicated
Put a number into another
Nightmare subject, nightmare subject.

Matthew Swallow (10)
Mayflower Primary School

I Wonder What Teachers Do?

Do they hate maths?
Do they like their job?
Do their cars run?
Are they cool or not?

Do they have a teddy bear?
Do they pick their nose?
Do they live in a mansion,
Or maybe down the road?

Do they party all night long?
Do they drink beer?
Do they party with other teachers?
Is pop music what they like to hear?

Can they dance?
Do they wear silly shoes?
Do they wear make-up?
I wonder what teachers do?

Georgia Houghton (10)
Mayflower Primary School

The Battle Of Marathon

I see silver swords glinting,
Maroon curdles with the blue seas,
Gulls diving sharp and swiftly,
Men fight for what they believe in.

I hear thundering feet charging,
Horses clomping their feet down,
Falls another man clashing,
Swords collide together.

I feel sick at the sight of this,
Terrible war is depressing everyone,
Feels that they are unwell,
And ill from this scene.

Laura Green (10)
Mayflower Primary School

Drawing

Drawing a picture,
Painting a picture,
Swishing and splashing on the soggy, wet paint,
Drawing on a picture,
Watching it march up and down on a piece of paper,
Painting a picture, drawing a picture,
Drawing a picture with pencil,
Painting over with paint,
Drawing is fun,
Painting is artistic,
Drawing a fab picture,
Getting all the attention,
Then make
A big mistake
And ruin
All the attention.

Sabrina Parsons (10)
Mayflower Primary School

My Silly, Loopy Teacher

My teacher's name is Mrs Loopy
She's very, very silly
And even though my brother is named Scott
She always calls him Billy.

My teacher is so weird
My teacher's mad and loopy
But when she's not mad anymore
She goes all droopy.

My teacher is so dopey
She is very, very mad
And when she starts to shout
It always makes you sad.

Abbie Elwood (10)
Mayflower Primary School

The Saucy Monster Under The Stairs

No one dares walk up them stairs
Because of the monster's den.
The monster only comes out at night
Because he gets a fright from the children.

He likes to eat tomato sauce
That he takes from the school kitchen,
So beware that you don't get squirted.

The deserted school grounds in the dusty morning,
The monster is still asleep,
So don't you dare, you better *beware!*
Because you might get eaten.

Eleanor Proctor (11)
Mayflower Primary School

All The Assemblies We Have

Assemblies are sometimes fun and sometimes boring,
Monday, Tuesday, Wednesday, Thursday are always early
                                                   in the morning,
There are always loads of kids around and naughty ones too,
No one hardly lets us go to the loo.

Assemblies smell of sweat, sometimes when we're hot,
There are loads of people around us and I mean a lot,
We fit the whole school in the hall,
When some classes are late we have to go and call.

Assemblies smell, sometimes really good,
It looks very wide and very big too,
It sounds loud when we sing,
It feels like everybody shouts at you.

Joanna Shields (11)
Mayflower Primary School

The Winding School Stairs

Up and down the winding stairs,
The more, the more you begin to care,
When stumbling you shed a tear,
In absolute fear.

Helping someone down the stairs,
Will let them know how much you care,
All along they'll know their true friend,
When you take care of them.

Listening to their problems,
They'll like you even more,
Because you're so sure,
That they'll like you.

Georgia Howell (11)
Mayflower Primary School

The Battle Of Marathon In A Different Way

I am a Greek soldier
I've got a shield and a sword
With all that bombing and fighting
I think, *oh good Lord!*

There I was standing
Then it started to thunder
Who invented fighting and battling
I wonder?

The next day the battle began
And there I was dead
Lying there all alone
Stabbed in the head.

Jack Copping (10)
Mayflower Primary School

Vampires

They are good,
They are bad,
They are very, very mad.

They are spooky,
They are scary,
They are very, very deadly.

They are talented,
They are hated,
They will disappear to kill.

They are swift,
They are not real,
They are really, really frightening.

Peter Howell (9)
Mayflower Primary School

Stairs

Some are winding
Some are long
Some are moving
Some are strong

Some are indoors
Some are out
Some have railings
Some without

Made of concrete
No one cares
They're important
They are stairs.

Daryl Whiffing (10)
Mayflower Primary School

Graffiti

Talented artists
Go around town
Heading for the skate park
They execute *graffiti* at night
People go mad
And the artists feel proud
Then there's a problem going around the massive city.

                        Graffiti is evil
                        It's really unpleasant
                        You can get in terrible danger
                        If you get caught
                        You'll be chased by the police
                        Artists think they're dudes
                        But they're a disgrace to the city
                        And they're rude.

The police go mad
And they feel distressed
They'll deal with the graffiti
And will take it seriously
You'll get arrested
Then your life will be *hell!*

Ryan Heath (10)
Mayflower Primary School

Germs

Germs can be good,
Germs can be bad,
They're multiplying in the air as we speak,
So be careful,
They can infect,
They can cause you lots of hassle, with unpleasant nights,
You can't see them so they can strike at any time,
So watch your backs, they're right behind you.

Naomi Edgar (11)
Mayflower Primary School

My Sister

My sister is trouble
My sister is a pest
Annoying me is her favourite
And simply her best.

My sister is untidy
She drives me up the wall
But really she's OK
And not bad after all.

My sister is kind
My sister is funny
I'm so relieved when she goes outside
To play when it's hot and sunny.

At the end of the day
I suppose she's OK
I wouldn't know what I would do without her.

Sophie Scott (10)
Mayflower Primary School

What Am I?

I am very small,
Not very tall,
I can hurt you,
I can heal you,
I can drive you up the wall,
I can multiply myself,
You can call me a bug,
But one that is not visible,
I am afraid of boiling water.

I am a microbe!

Thomas Denney (10)
Mayflower Primary School

Walking To School

Strolling to school, hop past the dog
Nearly through the hall
Sorry Mum, no hugs today
Squeeze through the door, kick the ball

Creep down the road
Take a right
Then a left
Avoid seeing the teacher in sight

At the playground
Catch my mate
Bell rings
Here lies my fate.

Paisley Tedder (10)
Mayflower Primary School

Germs

I can be good, I can be bad,
I will infect,
But you will not see me,
Because I am so tiny,
And out of reach.
I will go in and out your mouth all day,
Child from child,
Causing coughs and chest infections,
But . . .
Sometimes when I'm really bad,
I give you a disease!

Tiger Love (11)
Mayflower Primary School

Horses

Pale palomino, coat's twinkling in the sun,
A new friendship with a horse has only just begun.
A gleaming body brushed, made of gold and silver,
Horses drinking and watching water flowing down the river.
Speeding through courses and 2 foot 3 jumps,
Racing down hills on cold days gives me the goosebumps.
After a long ride put the rug on tight,
Then bolt the stable door and tell the horse goodnight.
Early in the morning, trudging through the mud,
My hands are so cold and numb they start pouring with blood.

Jemma Free (10)
Mayflower Primary School

Harwich

The beautiful beach
The lovely scenery
And the historic stories that the old men tell
And the beach is full of joy.

Ben Tedder (10)
Mayflower Primary School

My Best Friend

My best friend is the best at playing football.
He is good playing with my PS2 on Lord Of The Rings.
He's affectionate to all his friends and very understanding.
His is the best friend.
He helps small children when they are being bullied.

Callum Miller (10)
Mayflower Primary School

FA Cup - Manchester United Vs Liverpool

Whistle screeches, match starts
Manchester United in control
Rooney on the left
Lobs the ball down field into the 8 yard box
Intercepted by Joesmi
Out for a corner
Giggs swings it in, C Ronaldo headers it in to the top left hand corner
Goal!
Dudek couldn't get anywhere near that
That was just tremendous play by C Ronaldo
Liverpool take centre
Cisse whips it forward
What a mistake by Carrol
Morientes swipes it with the left foot, *goal!*
The equaliser, 1 minute into stoppage time in the first half
The half-time whistle blows and the score is 1-1
The managers are giving an influential team talk
The second half starts
Back to Ferdinand and then back to Carrol
Carrol hits it forward
Into the feet of Rooney
He whacks it into the bottom right hand corner, *goal!*
2-1 to Manchester United
Liverpool take centre once again
Scholes steals it and runs into the box
He's been pulled down by Hyypia
A penalty has been awarded to Manchester United
V Nistelrooy steps up, he shoots, he scores, what a *goal!*
That was stupendous
Full-time, Manchester United 3 Liverpool 1
Manchester United lift the sparkling, shiny, silver FA Cup!

Lloyd Beeney (11)
Mayflower Primary School

Friends

Friends should be funny
And never ever mad
They should be friendly
And should never break up.

If they fight or argue
You should walk away
Make a new friend
And stay with them.

Friends should share secrets
Otherwise they aren't your friends
They should be kind and entertaining
And they should be close, very close.

Friends should be like fish in the sea.

Kelly Chatterton (11)
Mayflower Primary School

A Witch's Poem

Twisting, turning, what a wonderful life,
Swiftly swooping through the moonlight.
Gliding through clouds,
Leaving a mist behind,
Diving in and out
To reach the next point.

You see the housetops
High up above,
Whizzing with the wind
Just like a bird.
Stars zooming around your head,
How I wish I could be up there.

Amelia Gooding (10)
Mayflower Primary School

The Fierce Dragon

Teeth glinting in the sun
Claws like razor-sharp metal
Eyes like bright red fire
Scales like razors.

Tail like a snake
Horns like pure, shiny gold
Circles of pure red rubies on his wings
Breath like rotten antelope's.

Yasmeen Amber (9)
Mayflower Primary School

Poem About Dancing

Dancing around in circles,
Around, around we go,
You feel like a bird swaying through the sky,
Swirling around the room,
Like a butterfly diving in some flowers,
Tap-tap-tap dance up and down,
Tap-tap-tap dance left and right,
Twirl, twirl, twirl your partner left and right,
Finish.

Bethany Slater (10)
Mayflower Primary School

Friendship

A friend is someone who is always there for you
and never ever leaves you out.
A friend is someone who will share secrets with you.
A friend is someone who would never talk about bad things
behind your back.
A friend is someone who plays with you every day.

Hayley Walker (10)
Mayflower Primary School

Birdy

Birds, birds
Fly so high
Shines so brightly
In the sky.

Pecking worms
Is what they do
And beetles
And other creatures too.

A bird's worst enemy
Is the cat
But they only get better
At being fat.

Worms in fear
Of when birds strike
When they see them
They say, 'Oh crike!'

Birds fly
Really high
Blazing like a star
As they're flying by.

Birds, birds
Fly south
In the winter nights
And they get frostbite.

Jordan Rodger (9)
Mayflower Primary School

Friendship

Sharing secrets and dreams,
Making your friends laugh and sing,
Gossiping loudly,
Jumping wildly,
Having a friend to talk to who is very delightful,
They can be very nasty,
But they're mostly nice to me,
That's why friendship is so great.

Hannah Coleman (10)
Mayflower Primary School

Tiger Poem

Black and orange, sharp killing claws,
Atrocious roaring for ears that hear,
Camouflaging into trees, ready to strike,
Argh!
Ripping flesh, blood's on the floor,
Other tigers smell blood, a fight begins,
Clawing, slashing, struggles to keep the dead body near,
Misses target, no longer one body on the floor but five!

Kiana Knight (10)
Mayflower Primary School

Tiger

The bright orange stripy tiger
Walking through the sun
Here comes his friend Liger
Having a little fun.

Jade Paice (10)
Mayflower Primary School

England Vs Croatia

England to kick off
Gerard to Beckham
Beckham to Neville
Neville back to the keeper
He boots it out to Owen
Owen crosses it
Goal!
Wayne Rooney.

Croatia to take centre
Their pass is intercepted
Beckham, that's a free kick
Beckham takes
Goal!
England in control.

Croatia straight on the attack
Into the edge of the area
Corner
It swings in
Goal!
2-1 to England.

England on the attack
Out for a corner
Beckham takes
Goal!
Frank Lampard scores.

3-1 to England
The ref is checking his watch
Full-time
3-1 to England.

Max Garnier (11)
Mayflower Primary School

A Match To Remember

Henry and Reyes are taking centre at Highbury,
The match begins.
Arsenal are in control of the ball.
Campbell passes to Cole,
Cole gives it to Henry.
He shoots - *goal!*
Great start for The Gunners -
Howard had no chance,
The crowd are going wild!
Centre for United,
Van Nistelrooy is with the ball - he shoots . . .
Good save by Lehmann.
Corner.
Giggs crosses it -
Goalkeeper punches it away.
Arsenal have possession,
Henry swings it for a cross -
Reyes scores!
The crowd are singing, '2-0 to The Ar-se-nal!'
Motson: 'What a goal!'
McCoist: 'A match to remember.'
Half-time.
Man U kick off.
Ronaldo passes to Giggs,
He has a shot . . . off the bar.
But what is happening?
Lehmann has made a bad mistake,
He has kicked the ball into his own net!
2-1 . . . whistle . . . full-time . . .
A match to remember.

Tom Goldsmith (11)
Mayflower Primary School

The Beauty Of Colour

Blue . . .
Desirous, dainty blue,
Flooding, carefree,
A swarm of red,
Blood, indigo, maroon, crimson and red,
Dying.
Green . . .
Envious green,
Threatened by others,
Gracious green,
Standing proud.
Yellow . . .
Glistening yellow,
Clashing with others,
Big-headed.
Purple . . .
Darkening mauve,
Lightning flashes,
Doom.
Orange . . .
Gleaming orange,
Sunshine, golden,
Brightening up life.

Emma Smith (10)
Parsons Heath CE Primary School

Shark

Shark
Was darker
Than fog.
Slices through
The deep ocean,
Eyes as red as
Rubies
That are fixed
Onto its prey.
Tail slashing
Through the water,
Gaining speed.
Jaws ready to
Sink into its food.

Shark
Was evil
That ruled the ocean,
For it glided
Over the seabed,
And filled the ocean
With fear.

Shark glided, fishes froze,
Splash - splash - *splash!*

Charlotte Holmes & George Clarke (11)
Parsons Heath CE Primary School

Mysterious Place

Cool, unsuccessful blue,
Washing over your mind.
Maze you can't get around.
Investigate new worlds.
Linking together,
Magnificent pink,
To sweeping, luxurious gold.

Spirals all around you,
Boxing you into an evil trap.
Don't know where to go.
Fossil like black,
Curling all over.
Lines here and there.
Straight and crinkly,
But twisting about.
Help me please,
To get out.
I really don't know my whereabouts.

Charlotte Chubb (10)
Parsons Heath CE Primary School

Pattern World In My Eyes

Sahara Desert is star-attracter.
Red Sea poisons sky beauty.
Royal Navy invades grassy fields.
Colour-cross, gifts, diamond king.
Mountains-dull dwell further east.
Colourful western stays in joy-world-happiness.
Navy Antarctica glistens down south.
Beautiful world lives on and on.
Shapes live all over the world.
The world is a rainbow ball.
This is the world in my eyes.

Jack McKenna (10)
Parsons Heath CE Primary School

An Underground Of Colours

A winter's midnight with bolts of electric yellow,
An ocean of melted rubies, flowing,
Spiders' cobwebs of metallic steel,
Scales of chocolate-brown,
Poisonous purple,
A mixed bag of sapphire seas,
Opaque emerald-green.

An Atlantic Ocean of indigo-blue,
Red gems diving beneath it,
A sailor's skin gleaming on the waves,
Thunder gold working with leaf-green,
Pyramids,
Outstanding, show-off orange.

Eyebrows of glistening, starless nights,
Jewels of shiny greens and browns,
Marching away into the distance.

Kelvin Yeung (11)
Parsons Heath CE Primary School

Winter

My hair is as white as frost on a winter's morning.
My icy eyes are coloured but clear.
My frozen face is the fog in the early air.
My teeth are the little droplets of dew on every lawn.
My frosty smell is the smell of fresh snowy fields.
When I cough my wind sends chills down spines.
I can move as quickly as thundering hailstones.
But I sometimes creep slowly, freezing the world in my path.
If you tasted me I would be a strong, sour peppermint.
My clothes are torn and tattered by the power of my presence.
My feet produce sleet as I kick the air.
My cold hands wrap around the seasons . . .
Winter.

Mitchell Attwood (11)
Parsons Heath CE Primary School

Winter

Raw, like an ice cube in your mouth,
Feathery snow tickles you,
Cold rain gives me frostbite,
Horrible blizzards blow me away,
Indoor fires toast my toes.

Freezing snow makes my fingers numb,
Icy mountains moan,
A whistling wind goes by,
The sound of tyres squeak across the ice,
Plump snowmen are like snow statues.

Its shining white face smiles,
Warm children play in the big field of white,
Inside children wait for St Nick,
A tree full of white sticks up like a hand,
    Winter is *here!*

Aidan Ware (10)
Parsons Heath CE Primary School

Winter

She moves slowly like a flourish of snow,
And sings her song in a frosty voice.
She has a raw look,
And if you touch her your fingers will freeze.
She has curly white hair like the pale sun,
She has a colourless face like a small cloud,
Piercing white eyes like an evil sorcerer's,
Pale skin like frost on the window,
And nails like ice on a hard lake.
She smells damp like rain,
And lemony like a sweet.
The ragged clothes on her like snow settled on a field,
A glacial mouth like chilly mountains . . .
She passes by . . .
And leaves a sprinkle of frost.

Alice Byford (10)
Parsons Heath CE Primary School

Magical World

Yellow desert surrounded by a glistening topaz sea,
A twisted tornado, pink and blue,
Heat colour orange with strawberry spots,
Shiny green arrowhead washed away.

A silky, shiny purple amethyst hanging in a cave wall,
Stroppy red waiting to make the world sorrowful,
A smoky orange warming up our day,
Lost green emerald but will it be found?

Red-red pool of blood dripping down a sewer,
Luminous yellow banana skin,
Edible orange toffees ready to be eaten,
Purple blackberry being absorbed up,
Pink strawberry lights up a grey prison cell,
Green pattern similar to mould.

Jamie Boughton (11)
Parsons Heath CE Primary School

Winter

Cold, harsh air holding a whip of ice,
A fight between snow and hail,
The ground covered with a thick white blanket,
The cruel, ugly face of winter,
Wispy, brittle platinum-blonde hair,
Speaking a menacing, echoing voice,
The words permanently swirl in your head,
Smell of wet grass fills the air,
A river gushing in the gutter,
Winter laughs a deep laugh,
He sits back and watches the mayhem,
He sends snow to conquer the world,
Only to find out we enjoy it,
He's furious and fuming, he sends rain,
Everybody's miserable, his work is done.

Alex Partridge (11)
Parsons Heath CE Primary School

Remembrance

Poppies bring our memories back,
Of the people who lost their lives,
The sorrow of losing our friends,
Despair of family, despair of death.

Fathers went to fight in the war,
My father did too,
We were left in anxiety,
Would he ever come back?

So remember the death of the soldiers,
You may think it is weird,
But imagine if you lost someone,
Very close to you.

It was a time of sadness,
Worry and despair,
So have a minute of silence,
And show that we care.

Emily Townsend (10)
Parsons Heath CE Primary School

My Pattern

A lightning bolt flashes
Through a stream of colours.
An ocean-like blue
Splashes on the page.
Ruby-red puzzle confuses
The mind.
A mind-numbing pattern
Of blue, red and green.

A snail shell empty and bare.
The plaque of gold filled
With sapphires.
Water falls from nowhere
Full of mysterious faces.

Bradley Orr (10)
Parsons Heath CE Primary School

Winter

The angry wind swirls through the winter's night.
Shiny stars brighten up the cold and frosty night,
Like the fire in the warm and cosy house.
The wind's howl is the croaky voice of an old man,
As white as a woolly sheep.
A frosty blanket covers the land.
Ice covers the glistening water.
The crystal clear ice smashes like glass being shattered.
Melting snow like a dripping ice cream.
Silky-white hair like the snow falling from the air.
Smoke floating in the air like the wind swaying.
Snowmen stand still like a tree covered in snow.
People in their cosy beds.
The dark night lays still.
The frosty ice melts away when the sun starts to rise.

Rosie Watts (10)
Parsons Heath CE Primary School

A Rainbow Pattern

Blue swirls that look like rats' tails,
Strips of rainbow colours, shooting stars,
Zigzags, tigers' fangs,
Purple stripes, spines of a hedgehog,
V-shapes, arrowheads,
Point to the green corner.

Polka dots on grassy green,
Square diamonds, triangles have different colours,
Stain-glass windows filled with so much joy.

Claws green, monsters' hands, orange nails,
Put it together and you have . . .
A rainbow pattern.

Sophie Davies (10)
Parsons Heath CE Primary School

Playpen

The sapphire-blue
Lying in the rocks.
Bloody-red flows
In the lake.
Ultramarine-blue
Marches.
Ruby-red in
The flames.
Leaf-green
Shining.
Sunshine-orange
With smiles.
Fire-red.
Steel-grey
With white smiles.
Leather bike-brown
With diamonds.
Royal-red
Clocks.
Lovely purple
Stripes.
Flame-red
Lines with
Orange.

Joshua Goodings (10)
Parsons Heath CE Primary School

Winter

Ice hangs from the windows,
like hardened, spiked hair.
Frozen over pools of ice,
like lonely pale blue eyes.
Sharp axe to cut wood for the fire,
like a pointed, cold nose.
The wind strikes you down,
like a shrieking voice.
The rawness of the night,
like the frost of a heart.
Sticks captured in ice,
like a woman's icy arms.
The freezing wind rushes through you,
like someone dashing to win a race.
This pale woman stands and stares,
wearing her gown of pure white.
A mole trapped underground,
like her frown stuck to her face.
Lumps of snow,
like her stubby toes.
Cracks in the ice,
like her broken heart.
Wind echoes through the night,
like the wails of a lonely ghost.
Spiderweb twigs,
like her spindly, long fingers.
She is alone, cold and miserable.

Evie Bolderson (11)
Parsons Heath CE Primary School

Creation

Freezing
Cold
Loneliness in the velvety black
A slow
Warming light appeared
A soft footstep
A splash of water
Smell of fresh air
Water glittering
In the sunlight.

Paul Byford (10)
Parsons Heath CE Primary School

Skeleton Dreaming

(Inspired by 'Fishbones Dreaming' by Matthew Sweeney)

The skeleton lay on the seabed
With bits of skin slowly floating off him
And colourful fish swimming past him with fright.

'He didn't like to be this way.
He shut his eyes and dreamed back'.

Back to when he was floating down in the water,
Struggling to breathe
And swim back up to the surface.

'He didn't like to be this way.
He shut his eyes and dreamed back'.

Back to when he was on his boat,
Someone pushing him off the boat in a temper.

'He didn't like to be this way.
He shut his eyes and dreamed back'.

Back to when he was on his boat happily
Looking for fish in the ocean with the sun warming his skin.

He liked to be this way.
He closed his eyes and tried to stay.

Alicia Foley (11)
R A Butler Junior School

The Arnolfini Marriage
(Inspired by Jan van Eyck's painting 'The Arnolfini Marriage')

Beside the sea a mansion stood,
The sound of shrieking gulls was clear,
On the morning of the marriage.

Inside the sleeping chamber, a bride gazed dreamily at her groom,
A candle burnt in the chandelier
On the morning of the marriage.

Through the door the guests were gathered,
The young dog's yapping was shrill,
On the morning of the marriage.

With the guests all watching, the bride and groom were wed,
The oranges trembled, an earthquake erupted,
On the morning of the marriage.

Beneath the rubble, the couple lay crushed,
The sound of gulls was clear,
On the day of the funeral.

Ella Hampson (11)
R A Butler Junior School

The Arnolfini Marriage
(Inspired by Jan van Eyck's painting 'The Arnolfini Marriage)

Among the bulb of a beautiful land,
At a palace of honour and pride
Stood a bride and groom in their wonderful room,
A merchant of wealth and a lady of life and beauty.

Many secrets of the past they held,
Of a dog and an all-seeing mirror.
Little did they know that in 600 year's time
They would be looked upon as interesting artefacts
Not as a good opportunity for a painting
And a bit of graffiti.

Sam Sawtell (10)
R A Butler Junior School

Skeleton Dreaming
(Inspired by 'Fishbones Dreaming' by Matthew Sweeney)

Skeleton lay at the bottom of the ocean
All scattered about,
With fish exploring his bones and getting stuck in his rib cage

'He didn't like to be this way.
He shut his eyes and dreamed back'.

Back to when he was sinking, struggling for breath,
Frantically trying to swim up to the surface,
His leg tangled in an old fish net.

'He didn't like to be this way.
He shut his eyes and dreamed back'.

Back to when he was on his ship, putting up the sail,
Fighting against a strong wind,
Calling helplessly to his mates; but no answer.

'He didn't like to be this way.
He shut his eyes and dreamed back'.

Back to when he was at home with his children,
His loving wife and a warm, blazing fire,
Eating a bit of cake on the sofa.

He liked it this way and wanted it to stay that way . . . forever.

Caitlin Jackson Corbett (11)
R A Butler Junior School

Christmas Thank Yous
(Based on 'Christmas Thank Yous' by Mick Gowar)

Dear Grandma,
Oh what a lovely bag,
Lilac, a colour so special to me,
And the beautiful embroidered flowers.
I absolutely adore the chain,
It hangs beside
My knee.

Dear Uncle,
Thanks for the Barbie,
Oh, how thoughtful of you.
I was crazy about them when I was younger,
You obviously haven't forgot,
Another one to my collection,
Now I have a few.

Dear Mum,
I love the electric guitar,
It feels like Heaven in my hand.
It looks and sounds fantastic,
Just ask the people next door.
I'm sure they won't complain as much
When I'm in a famous band.

Rebecca Watts (10)
R A Butler Junior School

Skeleton Dreaming
(Inspired by 'Fishbones Dreaming' by Matthew Sweeney)

A defenceless skeleton,
At the bottom of the ocean,
No skin, just bones,
Held in the waves' motion.
*'He didn't like to be this way,
He shut his eyes and dreamed back'.*

Sinking down, further and further,
Being tossed around by the rocks,
Trying to breathe, but not succeeding,
Sinking down from the docks.
*'He didn't like to be this way,
He shut his eyes and dreamed back'.*

Going overboard!
It was a scary fright,
He didn't know if he was going to live
And survive another night.
*'He didn't like to be this way,
He shut his eyes and dreamed back'.*

He remembered playing in the sun,
Playing on his red bike,
It was a lot of fun,
He wanted to stay, but he couldn't.
'He liked it this way,'
But he knew that he couldn't stay.

Alice Bol (10)
R A Butler Junior School

Skeleton Dreaming
(Inspired by 'Fishbones Dreaming' by Matthew Sweeney)

A nice, kind skeleton
At the bottom of the sea,
Lying there, just bones,
Only a bit of skin on his knee.

'He didn't like to be this way.
He shut his eyes and dreamed back'.

Floating down to the dark part of the sea,
All his skin,
Going down deeper,
Trying to breathe, eyes stinging.

'He didn't like to be this way.
He shut his eyes and dreamed back'.

Climbing up really high,
Standing on the look out,
Looking through the telescope,
Looking out for trouble.

'He didn't like to be this way.
He shut his eyes and dreamed back'.

Stepping on the boat with his friends,
Sailing away far out to sea,
Having lunch on the deck,
Playing with his friends.

He wanted to go back to the past.
He wanted to do those things again.

Trudi Saunders (10)
R A Butler Junior School

Skeleton Dreaming
(Inspired by 'Fishbones Dreaming' by Matthew Sweeney)

Skeleton lay at the bottom of the ocean,
In pitch-black without a head, he lay in mushy stuff.
*'He didn't like to be this way,
He shut his eyes and dreamed back'.*
He was in a submarine at work,
The alarm had just gone off,
And he was trying to save his own skin.
*'He didn't like to be this way,
He shut his eyes and dreamed back'.*
He was getting on to the submarine and saying goodbye to his son,
His son was crying because he didn't want his dad to go.
*'He didn't like to be this way,
He shut his eyes and dreamed back'.*
He was eating with his family happily,
With roast potatoes and tofu.
This is where he wanted to be,
He closed his eyes and tried to stay there.

Ned Harvey (10)
R A Butler Junior School

The Arnolfini Marriage
(Inspired by Jan van Eyck's painting 'The Arnolfini Marriage')

Beside the sea a palace stood,
Inside was a wedding,
Above the bride a chandelier hung,
With beautiful gold, one candle shone.

Opposite the bride, the groom stood,
Beside them their four-poster bed lay untouched,
From the ground it was covered in velvet,
Reflected in a gold-framed mirror.

Tom Carruthers (10)
R A Butler Junior School

Boy Flying
(Inspired by Leslie Norris)

Flying,
he smelt the greenness of the freshly mown grass,
picturing the lawn short and straight.
The sweet chocolatey aroma of his mum's most recent cake,
smoke spiralling up from next door's bonfire.
He inhaled the reek of wet dog, as the escaped victim ran barking
around the torturer's garden.

He could not smell the wafting perfume of the spring flowers,
nor the faint odour of ice cream, as the van trundled down the lane.

Flying,
he felt the candyfloss clouds, filled with small droplets of water,
spiralling down, he felt the cold sting of snowflakes as he danced
with them through the sky.
He felt the warm gust of smoke rising as he floated above the rooftops.
He suffered the sting of the unfriendly wind,
as it sent him whirling towards mountains.

He could not feel the softness of his kitten's fur.
He missed the warm nights in front of the fire, safe and sound.

Flying,
he saw the fluffy sheep, and the pretty young girl watching them.
He saw the wild expanse of grass, dotted by a few rabbit burrows.
He saw the red flash of fox's fur as the sly creature disappeared
amongst the purple heather.

Flying,
he heard the crunch and cracks of the leaves and the twigs
under the hunter's foot.
He heard the excited barking of his hunting dogs.
He heard the loud, clear gunshot and the screeches of protest
from the birds as they rose from the trees.

He could not hear anymore, nor smell, or feel or see,
as he plummeted from the sky.

Anna Dodge (10)
R A Butler Junior School

Skeleton Dreaming
(Inspired by 'Fishbones Dreaming' by Matthew Sweeney)

There he lay,
alone,
scattered in a heap.

'He didn't like to be this way,'
dreaming, dreaming, dreaming.

Falling down into the depths of the dark,
twirling and twisting,
round and round.

'He didn't like to be this way,'
dreaming, dreaming, dreaming.

On the plank,
taking pigeon steps to try
and make his pirate's life last longer.

'He didn't like to be this way,'
dreaming, dreaming, dreaming.

Talking to his friends,
and enjoying his life.

This is the way he wanted to be,
happy, happy, happy.

Emma Jenkins (11)
R A Butler Junior School

Skeleton Dreaming
(Inspired by 'Fishbones Dreaming' by Matthew Sweeney)

A skeleton was dreaming,
As he lay in the reeds of the sea.
A dream in the war,
It was he, as a man in the fight.

They were forced to the cliff edge,
Shooting, banging going on.
He shot and got shot
And went falling to his perilous doom.

As the sea came ever closer, he screamed.
No good, no one could save him now.
He hit the water with a splash.
He was drowning, down and down he went.

He slowly started to rot,
In the salty water.
Until he was nothing but bones,
As he lay there dead forever.

He didn't like to be this way,
As a pile of bones.
A skeleton was dreaming,
As he lay in the reeds of the sea . . .

Eddie Pottrill (10)
R A Butler Junior School

A Skeleton Dreaming
(Inspired by 'Fishbones Dreaming' by Matthew Sweeney)

A skeleton lying in the deep blue,
Bones everywhere and all mouldy,
Soon the fish would be making homes in his head.
'He didn't like to be this way.
He shut his eyes and dreamed back'.

To a body once with skin and clothes,
Sinking, not able to breathe,
Then hitting the sand with a bump.
'He didn't like to be this way.
He shut his eyes and dreamed back'.

To when the wave came and took him away,
When he was taken under and could not take one gulp of air.
'He didn't like to be this way.
He shut his eyes and dreamed back'.

Back to when he was on his lilo having great fun,
Enjoying his day at the beach.
He liked it this way.
He wanted to stay here but he knew he couldn't.

Lizzie Clark (10)
R A Butler Junior School

Boy Flying
(Inspired by Leslie Norris)

Flying,

He smelled the mouth-watering aroma of fish and chips,
mixed in with the intoxicating smell of petrol.

He sensed the presence of lemons and suddenly felt a
burst of hunger shoot at him, sending saliva up his throat.

He flew over the forest, peering over the wall of flames,
catching sight of a cornered squirrel, but he could do nothing.

On he went, back to his resting place, crying again.

Oliver Moktar (10)
R A Butler Junior School

Skeleton Dreaming
(Inspired by 'Fishbones Dreaming' by Matthew Sweeney)

Skeleton bones lay on the ocean floor,
Eventually there would be more and more.

'He didn't like to be this way.
He shut his eyes and dreamed back'.

Back to when he was bobbing along on the ocean surface,
His skin starting to crack.

'He didn't like to be this way.
He shut his eyes and dreamed back'.

Back to when he was flying through the air engulfed in flames,
The air filled with burning ashes.

'He didn't like to be this way.
He shut his eyes and dreamed back'.

Back to when he was in total control of the plane,
Swooping and flying freely through the air with the enemy in sight.

'He liked to be this way'.

Harry Stocking (10)
R A Butler Junior School

Warmth Of The Night
(Inspired by Walter de la Mare)

Night is as kind as the warmth in your house,
He is as comforting and as caring as your most loving toy,
I feel as safe as when I'm in my bed,
My cover over me, my pillow under my head,
My dreams are inviting, friendly and safe,
It is as if night is watching me and gone when I wake,
A smiling, trustworthy, caring face,
Big brown eyes and a long black cape,
Glittering stars and a gleaming moon,
Night is moving swiftly and softly,
Disturbing no one that's at peace in their own little world.

Jenny King (10)
R A Butler Junior School

Skeleton Dreaming
(Inspired by 'Fishbones Dreaming' by Matthew Sweeney)

Skeleton lay at the bottom of the sea,
All broken up and rotten,
Shrimps swimming in and out of the ribcage.
'He didn't like to be this way,
He closed his eyes and dreamed back'.

He was floating down to the bottom of the sea,
And while he was drowning he was trying to breathe,
He knew he was going to die.
'He didn't like to be this way,
He closed his eyes and dreamed back'.

He was eating his lunch on his boat,
And he didn't realise that he was about to crash,
He fell out and he started to drown.
'He didn't like to be this way,
He closed his eyes and dreamed back'.

He was back lying on the warm sand,
Playing with his family,
And playing in the sea,
Like it should be, he liked it this way.

Emily Bayford (10)
R A Butler Junior School

Snow

Snow
Melts on my glove
It's crumbly, soft and cold
Snow is as white as paper
And as soft as my pillow
It makes my fingers glow
Snow
I love it!

Anthony Waite (10)
R A Butler Junior School

Skeleton Dreaming
(Inspired by 'Fishbones Dreaming' by Matthew Sweeney)

Left alone, squashed in a corner between two big boulders;
head one side, body the other and legs nowhere to be seen.
Buried beneath the surface of living life.
'He didn't like to be this way.
He closed his eyes and dreamed back'.

Falling, falling.
Down deeper, deeper,
blown off the side of a ship. *Crash!*
Screaming and swimming as helpless as a baby,
drowned by the vicious current.
'He didn't like to be this way.
He closed his eyes and dreamed back'.

When he was in a group, playing with his friends,
laughing and playing all day.
Snuggling up in bed as warm as can be.
'He liked to be this way'.

Fraser Parry (10)
R A Butler Junior School

Gleaming Night
(Inspired by Walter de la Mare)

Night is a dream giver, it sends you off to sleep
With its cape of moon dust and sweet breath too.
Night is thoughtful,
Its muffled voice sings you off to sleep,
With its shining, bright, bright black eyes and long golden hair
Moving in the depths of the darkness.

Night is a vampire, its long, gleaming white fangs,
It makes you feel jumpy like there's something there, waiting,
With its dangerous red eyes and big black cape over its head,
His head is full of mist,
It haunts your nightmares like a ghost flying behind you.

Night is a dream giver, it sends you off to sleep.

Emily Smith (11)
R A Butler Junior School

Skeleton Dreaming
(Inspired by 'Fishbones Dreaming' by Matthew Sweeney)

Skeleton lying on the bottom of the ocean,
All parts of his body scattered,
Soon fish would be making homes in his head.

*'He didn't like to be this way
So he shut his eyes and dreamed back'.*

Back to when he was whole with skin and clothes,
Holding his breath trying to swim up,
But he was tied up on a piece of seaweed.

*'He didn't like to be this way
So he shut his eyes and dreamed back'.*

Back to when he slipped on some soap
And flipped over the edge
And hit the water with a big splash.

*'He didn't like to be this way
So he shut his eyes and dreamed back'.*

Back to when he was sailing along
Through calm waters,
Stopping to do a bit of fishing.

*'He liked to be this way
He dreamed harder to stay there'.*

Jai Goodwin (11)
R A Butler Junior School

Skeleton Dreaming
(Inspired by 'Fishbones Dreaming' by Matthew Sweeney)

His body lay there still and motionless,
Scattered about: no skin, just bones:
Not a pretty sight.
'He didn't like to be this way,
He shut his eyes and dreamed back'.

Back to when he was falling down,
Chunks of skin taken out of him,
The water going red as he fell to the seabed.
'He didn't like to be this way,
He shut his eyes and dreamed back'.

Back to when he tripped off the boat,
The shark lunging at him taking back the life he led
No choice of whether he lived or died.
'He didn't like to be this way,
He shut his eyes and dreamed back'.

Back to when he was with his wife,
Waking up to the smell of cooked bacon,
Her tender flesh against his face.
He liked it there,
He dreamed hard, trying to stay there.

Zoë Maskell (11)
R A Butler Junior School

Skeleton Dreaming
(Inspired by 'Fishbones Dreaming' by Matthew Sweeney)

Skeleton lay at the bottom of the ocean
Fish dashing in and out of his eye sockets
Most of his bones scattered everywhere.

*'He didn't like to be this way
He shut his eyes and dreamed back'.*

Back to when he was floating down
Down, down, down to the bottom of the sea
His eyes stinging in the salty water
His clothes wet and bedraggled
The sea forcing him down
Everything dark and gloomy

*'He didn't like to be this way
He shut his eyes and dreamed back'.*

Back to when he was on his boat
The sun shining bright
People waving and looking, happy to see him

'He liked to be this way'
He shut his eyes and tried hard to stay there.

Morgan Brooks (10)
R A Butler Junior School

Skeleton Dreaming
(Inspired by 'Fishbones Dreaming' by Matthew Sweeney)

Skeleton lay at the bottom of the sea,
All broken up and crumbled,
Fish used him as a lovely home.

*'He didn't like to be this way.
He shut his eyes and dreamed back'.*

Back to when he was floating down
And realised he was dying.
He wanted to breathe but couldn't.

*'He didn't like to be this way.
He shut his eyes and dreamed back'.*

He was practising dives,
A shark came and surprised him.

*'He didn't like to be this way.
He shut his eyes and dreamed back'.*

Back to when he worked in a fish store,
He loved working there,
He loved smelling like fish,
He loved the past.

Julia Marsden (10)
R A Butler Junior School

The Haunted House

This is the house on Braderly Street,
a house full of spirits who refuse to retreat.
This is the kitchen where the cook's often seen,
then she withers away with an ear-piercing scream.
This is the picture of a girl, sad and caring,
but even though she's a picture you feel like she's staring.
This is the garden where a dog's seen at night,
most people who have seen it have fainted of fright.
This is the driveway where a phantom coach stops,
it's old and it's rusty with its doors hanging off.
This is the house on Braderly Street,
a house full of spirits who refuse to retreat.
The owners surrendered, the house on its own,
so the cause of the haunting will never be known.

Alice Marks (10)
R A Butler Junior School

Skeleton Dreaming

(Inspired by 'Fishbones Dreaming' by Matthew Sweeney)

Skeleton lay at the bottom of the ocean,
His bones scattered far and wide.
'He didn't like to be this way
He shut his eyes and dreamed back'.
Back to when he was sinking down into the dark, gloomy sea
With just his skin left,
Water rushing through his body.
'He didn't like to be this way
He shut his eyes and dreamed back'.
Back to when he was in the navy, fighting for his country,
Fighting for glory until a blade pierced his body.
'He didn't like to be this way
He shut his eyes and dreamed back'.

Oliver Gramlick (10)
R A Butler Junior School

Skeleton Dreaming
(Inspired by 'Fishbones Dreaming' by Matthew Sweeney)

Down at the bottom of the ocean,
A body lay empty and open,
All that was left was a head and a ribcage.
'He didn't like to be this way.
He shut his eyes and dreamed back'.

Dreamed back to the time he had his skin, but was dead,
Floating softly to the bottom of the clear water,
For someone to come and find him.
'He didn't like to be this way.
He shut his eyes and dreamed back'.

Back to when he was plummeting down a cliff,
The wind rushing through his hair and the air feeling solid,
Losing a small amount of skin on the sharp rocks.
When he thumped down onto the sandy beach,
The incoming tide brushed him away.
'He didn't like to be this way.
He shut his eyes and dreamed back'.

Dreamed back to the time he was smiling,
Riding down the road on his bike,
Flashing past all his neighbours,
With no hands on the handlebars.
The wind rushing through his hair
And the air feeling solid.
Oh, he liked it this way
And he wanted to stay here, but he couldn't.

Lucy Breed (11)
R A Butler Junior School

Skeleton Dreaming
(Inspired by 'Fishbones Dreaming' by Matthew Sweeney)

Skeleton lay deep, deep down at the bottom of the ocean.
Bones spread out on the soft, soaking sand.
Fish swimming through the sockets of where the eyeballs would be.
Soon the bones would rot to the core.
As he lay at the bottom of the ocean,
he realised he didn't want to be here, so he dreamed back.

Sinking slowly through the current of the water,
getting more of a sensation to breathe.
It was too late to try to swim and nobody was trying to help him,
nobody knew he was there.
As he hit the sand he realised he didn't like it this way,
so he dreamed back.

Coming home from work, excited to see his loving wife and children.
Sitting by the fire, watching a movie, snuggled up together.
Having Sunday roast, sitting around the wooden table as a family.

As he ate his dinner he realised he loved it this way
and decided to try and stay there forever.

Tom Wass (11)
R A Butler Junior School

Skeleton Dreaming
(Inspired by 'Fishbones Dreaming' by Matthew Sweeney)

Skeleton lay in a dump, stuck there to rot away for years to come.
Waiting for the rats to fight over him.
Wanting to be found and be thrown back into the ocean.
'He didn't like to be this way.
He shut his eyes and dreamed back'.

Him, poor person, getting stuck in a human net.
Struggling, getting one step closer to dying every second.
'He didn't like to be this way.
He shut his eyes and dreamed back'.

On a frying pan, sizzling and spurting,
With a fish staring and glaring into his empty eye-holes.
Only a few more minutes until the meeting with his doom.
'He didn't like to be this way.
He shut his eyes and dreamed back'.

Swimming up and down in an endless ocean.
Happy at being free.
'He liked to be this way'
And wished that he had never been caught by the evil fish.
Just think how you would feel if you were caught?

Nick Fane (10)
R A Butler Junior School

Skeleton Dreaming
(Inspired by 'Fishbones Dreaming' by Matthew Sweeney)

Skeleton lying at the bottom of the sea
the skeleton wishes
he could be alive like the fishes.

Skeleton wishes that his dreams would come true
when . . .

. . . he would be falling through the ocean
just been blown up, dropping with no motion.

But he does not like that dream so
skeleton wishes that his dreams could come true
when . . .

. . . he was on a warship, cruising in the water,
when a submarine blew him up with heavy mortar.

But he does not like that dream so
skeleton wishes that his dreams would come true
when . . .

. . . he was sailing with a mate,
he was simply feeling great.

Danny Elstub (11)
R A Butler Junior School

Skeleton Dreaming
(Inspired by 'Fishbones Dreaming' by Matthew Sweeney)

Shark lies washed up on the beach
In a terrible state, with one fin missing.
'He didn't like to be this way
He shut his eyes and dreamed back'.

At the point of death he felt the hunters strike again,
Pulling his flesh and tugging at his brain.
He tried to fight back: but he failed.
The hunter's strike pierced him. Death.
'He didn't like to be this way
He shut his eyes and dreamed back'.

Swimming peacefully, looking for his prey,
Before the hunters came and took his life away.
'He didn't like to be this way
He shut his eyes and dreamed back'.

Swimming free, eating fish,
Swimming through the sea,
Chasing his friends around the ocean bed.
'He liked to be this way'
He dreamed hard to stay in the ocean.

Ryan Martin (10)
R A Butler Junior School

Skeleton Dreaming
(Inspired by 'Fishbones Dreaming' by Matthew Sweeney)

Skeleton lay at the bottom of the ocean,
The sharks had been at him and he lay there
Feeling hopeless and lonely.
Bones were scattered randomly throughout the sandy sea.

*'He didn't like to be this way,
He shut his eyes and dreamed back'.*

The waves rocked him backwards and forwards,
The stinging in his eyes was painful
And everywhere he looked was a big blur.
He'd held his breath for as long as he could . . .
Until he could no longer.

*'He didn't like to be this way,
He shut his eyes and dreamed back'.*

Having fun on his boat,
The sudden, *huge* gust of wind.
Toppling overboard,
There were shouts, screams and cries of sadness.

*'He didn't like to be this way,
He shut his eyes and dreamed back'.*

Having a great time with his friends, fishing,
The sun beamed down on his face
And small, refreshing splashes sprayed his body,
Free and happy,
He wanted to stay like this forever.

He liked it this way and he didn't have to dream . . .

Zoë Lett (11)
R A Butler Junior School

The Arnolfini Marriage
(Inspired by Jan van Eyck's painting 'The Arnolfini Marriage')

Beneath the window sill of a palace was a dark, dingy moat,
Inside that palace was a wedding.
Between the bride and the groom was a dog.
Behind them all was a mirror.
Within the mirror was a reflection looking back at them.
Hanging from the ceiling was a chandelier.
Next to the chandelier was a four-poster bed.
Over the four-poster bed hung a velvet damask curtain.
On the floor was a red Turkish carpet.
Beside the wall was a pair of patterns.
Upon the groom was a hat.
Above the barometer was graffiti.
The graffiti said *'van Eyck was here!'*

William Lockton (10)
R A Butler Junior School

The Goblin's Cellar

The rusty cellar and the silky cobwebs
Hanging from the splintered ceiling
Smell of rotten animal shells
Squashed on the filthy floor
Dusty, burnt wood lying on the melted table
The tasteless food
Splattered across the freezing ice-covered walls
Spiders feasting and scampering on it
Sounds of frozen water
Breaking from the gloomy tap
Feel the cold, blistering air
If I were you
I wouldn't dare to enter
Or even stare.

Lizzie Bailey (8)
St Andrew's CE Primary School, North Weald

Chocolates

C hewy and sweet
H ere they are, a treat
O range cream
C oconut supreme
O pen up your mouth
L ovely sweet mouse
A surprise in a wrapper
T ongue-twisting cracker
E verything is great
S neak before it's too late.

Kaylee Orchard (10)
St Andrew's CE Primary School, North Weald

Goosebumps

They're frightening and scary
The monsters are hairy.
They're much too scary!
There are monsters and mummies,
They make you want to scream.
You better beware
They'll give you a scare.

Jason Caffrey (9)
St Andrew's CE Primary School, North Weald

Shark

S avage killer
H orrid hunter
A ggressive fighter
R avaging eater
K iller animal.

Thomas Southgate (10)
St Andrew's CE Primary School, North Weald

Homework

H orrid homework
O f course it's boring
M y brain shouldn't be doing maths and
E nglish after school.
W ish I could flush it down the loo
O r my dog could eat it
R ubbish stuff and it always feels like it's going to
K ill me.

George Sykes (10)
St Andrew's CE Primary School, North Weald

Dolphin

D ancing in the sea,
O n the bottom of the ocean,
L ovely to watch,
P erfect in every way,
H orrible when provoked,
I nteresting and fun,
N ice to watch,
S wimming in the sea.

Lacey Marie Payton (11)
St Andrew's CE Primary School, North Weald

Grandad

G randad is the best
R emember, not like the rest
A lways takes me out
N ever ever shouts
D oing lots of things
A n amazing grandad
D ogs are his favourite animals.

Kelly White (10)
St Andrew's CE Primary School, North Weald

Coming And Going To School

I opened the gate to my fate
Going to school,
I'm a fool but cool with my uncle.
He eats my chips then he flips
With sugar on his lips.
Round the corner
Towards the sauna, but no,
There's my aunt Lorna.
Up the hill it kills,
And there's my mate Phil.
At school, Green Lane, I find fame.
At school it's cool
The bell rings, I sing.

Coming home from school, all alone,
With my phone and a cool ringtone.
Down the hill with my mate Phil,
There's the corner, still no sauna.
There's my house,
Can't wait to see my mouse.
Bye I'm in my house.

Charlie Holloway (10)
St Andrew's CE Primary School, North Weald

Guess Who?

B eautiful in all ways with
U nbelievable colours
T iny legs
T otally perfect
E xcellent flyers
R emarkable tongues
F un to play with
L ovely wings
Y ummy layers of pollen.

Lauren Barrett (10)
St Andrew's CE Primary School, North Weald

The Goblin's Cellar

Children are in cages
Somebody's parts in jars
The children's little teddy bears
And some of their broken cars
Dusty cobwebs on the walls
Cold drip-dropping taps
A big stone door with two guards beside it
And two very fierce white cats
Spiders crawling everywhere
Fire burning hot
Grubby ceiling to match the floor
And more for it to rot
So that's the story of the goblin's cellar
Oh I mustn't forget the soggy umbrella
Shout out hooray, the children break free
Do not invite that goblin for tea!

Tillie Merritt (9)
St Andrew's CE Primary School, North Weald

Disco

Leaving school
So excited
Can't wait to see my friends in lovely clothes
Got home
Went in a roasting shower
Then I found my great outfit
Ready to go to the disco!
Got in the car, drove back to the school
Saw my friends in funky clothes
Went in school to the disco
I danced
I ate delicious food
Then I went home.

Samantha Gallacher-Bright (8)
St Andrew's CE Primary School, North Weald

Tracy Beaker

Tracy Beaker is the best
and she beats all the rest.

Tracy in a dump
and she has a big, big hump.

Justine Littlewood did a whine
but Tracy just did a sign.

Louise had a big, big wound
but Tracy just went straight to her room.

Justine Littlewood was in charge
but Tracy just looked at her and barged.

Justine and Louise went to bed
but Tracy hit them on the head.

Justine Littlewood went to say hi
but Tracy just said bye.

Tracy's mum went for a visit
and Tracy went to list it.

Emily Thomasz (7)
St Andrew's CE Primary School, North Weald

Disco

Leaving school, really excited
Looking forward to seeing friends in groovy outfits
Want to look my very best
Getting my outfit on
It's the poshest outfit in my wardrobe
Walking back to St Andrew's School
Can see friends in beautiful clothes
Can't wait to start dancing on the dance floor
Been dancing a lot, can't stop!
Going home now, had a great time
Got memories of tonight in my head.

Lauren Huff (8)
St Andrew's CE Primary School, North Weald

Disco

I'm leaving school
I'm feeling really happy
I can't wait for the
Disco later on today
Got to go home
And change my clothes
Still don't
Know what to wear
Who knows?
At home now, changing my clothes
Wearing jeans and a top to go, so let's go!
Walking back with friends
Seeing them in lovely clothes
Still can't wait
Am I early
Or late?

Jack Holloway (8)
St Andrew's CE Primary School, North Weald

The Witch's Kitchen

The big spell pot
With poison frogs and slimy snakes.
The black cat on the table, spying for intruders
For the witch to eat up.
Don't forget the bats
You may not see
Because they are hiding in the dark corner
Waiting for blood to suck.
From the kitchen window you can see
The dark, rocky gravestones.
The bright orange pumpkin head
Gleaming in the kitchen.

Daniel Neat (9)
St Andrew's CE Primary School, North Weald

Chocolate Crazy

C runchy caramel
H appy children slurping chocolate
O range chocolate with a taste
C hocolate biscuits in a tin
O range, mint, fruit and nut, so much to choose
L ate at night causes nightmares
A te it for breakfast, ate it for lunch, now I'm about to eat it for tea
T erry's Chocolate Orange goes down the back of my throat
E veryone messy, everyone happy, thanks to yummy chocolate.

Lewis Sibley (10)
St Andrew's CE Primary School, North Weald

The Witches' Kitchen

The bubbling cauldron
With air that is so thick
You cannot breath in it.
They are chanting, 'Doom doom!'
To all that enter.
The oozing blood out of the cauldron.
The black cat.
Cobwebs hanging from the mouldy ceiling.

Alec Pike (9)
St Andrew's CE Primary School, North Weald

Babies

B abies are cute.
A lways crying.
B ehaving nicely.
I see you baby.
'E llo little baby.
S weet dreams.

Luke Carrington (10)
St Andrew's CE Primary School, North Weald

The Inventor's Workshop

A rusty, old, broken mechanical car
In the corner on its side.
A dusty workbench
With cobwebs aside like frozen worms.
Gigantic spiders spinning a sticky web.
A broken clock with rotten feather hands
On a bent clock face.
An old, rotting fireplace
With a fire that is still burning, his latest invention
A splintered old toolbox,
With broken tools inside.

James Gomez (8)
St Andrew's CE Primary School, North Weald

The Aliens' Spacecraft

The aliens' incredible technology is surprising
But whatever you do don't get caught
For their torture chamber's terrible
It's full of thick, runny blood.
You shall see the aliens' freaky heads
Full of brilliant, strange, unusual knowledge.
Then the engine room
Full of silent technology with fantastic horsepower.

Daniel Gooderham (8)
St Andrew's CE Primary School, North Weald

The Alien Spacecraft

The cracked teleportation device,
Twinkling plasma rifle.
Old, rusted stand that could snap,
The crooked bone-crushing door.
A royal suite that is hung by a human finger.

Jack Osborne (8)
St Andrew's CE Primary School, North Weald

The Monster's Cave

The black, dark, gooey, grimy ceiling
With broken off claws on the floor.
The gross, horrible rats, mice, bats
Flying and scampering all round the cave.
Broken, flattened, rusty cars,
Just nothing left of them.
Slimy parts of the body kept in little glass jars.
Red blood soaked on the walls and floors.
Be careful of him, he isn't much fun.
He'll squash you to pieces,
You can be sure of that.
He drools green splodgy goo all from his mouth.
It's like living in a bubbling cauldron.
So stay away from the monster's cave
Otherwise you just might get a fright!

Jamie Fall (8)
St Andrew's CE Primary School, North Weald

The Witch's Kitchen

On top of the door
There was a black cat
With two green eyes
When people walked in
It would *hiss!*
The cauldron was empty
Then it was full
The broomstick jumped
Into the cauldron then stirred
To the left and to the right
Then jumped out
The bat flew around the room
The hat got scared of the bat
And jumped into the cauldron.

Amy Mohr (9)
St Andrew's CE Primary School, North Weald

The Inventor's Workshop

As people open the door the doorbell rings
You can hear the potions' bubbles and bings
Potions, so colourful and bright
They shine deep in the night
A wooden table, a wooden stall
Cobwebs all over the wall
Never go there, if you dare
Because you are going in his spooky lair.

Charlotte Levy (9)
St Andrew's CE Primary School, North Weald

The Witch's Kitchen

The rusty cauldron stood in a plain, dark corner of the dark kitchen.
The dark shadow of the broomstick was there on the wall.
The pointy hat, with the black cat sleeping with its dark green eyes.
The spell books stood on the cobwebbed shelf
With great big black spiders hanging onto the shelf.
The dusty cloak that the witch wears is hanging on the door
On a rusty, metal hook.
The spidery clock hangs on the wall.

Beth Sibley (9)
St Andrew's CE Primary School, North Weald

The Witch's Front Room

The cauldron smells like sewers in front of the smoky, black fire
There are dead animals lying on the floor in blood
The witch walks through the red, horrible blood
In the corner of the room are rotten, old, broken witches' brooms
And on the chair full of hairs a red-eyed, black cat is staring at you.

Jordan Albert (8)
St Andrew's CE Primary School, North Weald

Hariet The Hedgehog

This is Hariet
We found her in the garden
Brown and shy
I wonder why
She was probably
Hungry
Poor old thing
Needing to be fed
So we gave her some bread
Hariet is an animal, have you guessed what?
Well, figure it out.

Rebecca Wheeler (9)
St Andrew's CE Primary School, North Weald

Moment

Dirty dustbins
Clinking and clanking
Skinny cats
Miaowing and purring
Hunting for food.

Rebecca Cole (8)
St Andrew's CE Primary School, North Weald

The Alien Spacecraft

In the sky I see a ship
It is marvellous and clean like a shooting star
I saw a control panel like a remote control
It was as tall as one thousand houses put together
It was hard and big as a shooting rocket.

Adam Berwick (8)
St Andrew's CE Primary School, North Weald

Mum's China

Mum has fifty china plates,
All with different patterns
Most of which is bordered in Latin.

Mum has a special cutlery set
Bought by my mum's mum
When the set is out, there's not another crumb.

Mum has many china things
They really drive me mad
When she gets one for Christmas
She always says, 'That one's not bad!'

Katie Mehew (9)
St Andrew's CE Primary School, North Weald

The Explorer's Attic

The spooky attic is filled with cobwebs and spiders
With a cracked ceiling in the top of the spooky attic.
A fat, scary man stands at the door of the attic
Waiting for someone to come
He says, 'What are you doing here?'

David Paterson (9)
St Andrew's CE Primary School, North Weald

The Witch's Kitchen

Into the witch's kitchen, there's a creaking door
Patterned cobwebs on the stone ceiling and dust on the creaking floor
Scary spiders on the wooden wall at every dusty corner
And I couldn't forget about the cooking cauldron
Out of the scary kitchen, I had a nice time
And I didn't mention about the sticky slime.

Lucy-Ann Phillips (9)
St Andrew's CE Primary School, North Weald

Trebuchets

A relative of a catapult
As heavy as an elephant.

As dangerous as a tiger
As long as a snake.

As big as a house
As hard as wood.

Ropes as strong as metal
Wood as hard as concrete.

As old as the imperial ages
As slow as a seal
With bombs as big as footballs.

Daniel Mallett (9)
St Andrew's CE Primary School, North Weald

Sun

As hot as a volcano, bubbling lava
Hotter than a steaming kettle
Bigger than the Earth which gives up lots of space
Bigger than the shining moon which gives us light
In fact, it is the biggest thing in the universe.

Eloise White (9)
St Andrew's CE Primary School, North Weald

Whale

It is as big as can be
And it lives in the sea
Its mouth is as big as a black hole
It is as blue as the sky
It finds krill very tasty
And is as wet as a hundred flannels.

Lee Goody (9)
St Andrew's CE Primary School, North Weald

Tigers In The Wild

The sun shines as bright as it can on the tiger's silky back
His stripes as black as coal, even if he is in the sun
His long teeth glisten in the sun as white as snow
It brings fear to everybody's soul
His hunting skills are as good as a cheetah chasing deer or antelope
A shiver runs down everybody's back as he's just about to spring
I duck
He doesn't want to eat me, he just wants a drink of crystal clear water.

Stevie Smithson (9)
St Andrew's CE Primary School, North Weald

Rock Concert

A sound from your mouth blazing out
A sound as soft as a cloud
A rocking song with rhythm very loud
Elvis had a big crowd
The crowd would not stop cheering
Then there were fists flying
Legs swinging, but
Some still cheering at the end of the night.

Alfie Russell (9)
St Andrew's CE Primary School, North Weald

Trees

As hard as a table
As rusty as an old car
As big as a killer whale
As brown as a bear
As green as grass
As tall as a giraffe
What can it be?

Reece Donoghue (9)
St Andrew's CE Primary School, North Weald

Cheetah

There's an antelope in front of you
I know what you're going to do
You're going to jump on it in surprise
And rip it up until it dies.

Then bring it back to your lair
And eat with other cheetahs there
Under the tree that's where you'll lay
And until dinner that's where you'll stay.

Evening comes and evening goes
The next day is when you rose
You open up your sleeping eye
How many animals today will die?

Sam Berwick (9)
St Andrew's CE Primary School, North Weald

Aliens

A slimy, black creature roaming the stormy wasteland of its
                                        home planet of LV-426
It fights the storm for home and shelter
There is a food shortage because of stormy conditions
He has to shelter in rocky crevices.

Matthew Wheatley (9)
St Andrew's CE Primary School, North Weald

Clouds

As light as a feather
falling from the sky above the countryside
As fluffy as a white pillow
staying in the sky, not coming down for a while
As white as snow
smoothly gliding through the top of the sky
Going as fast as a tortoise.

Ben Warren (9)
St Andrew's CE Primary School, North Weald

Moment

Walking in the park
In the snow
All silent
Watching my dog
Fetching his ball
Suddenly
A group of children come
All screaming
I give one my ball
She plays with my dog.

Scarlett Stock (8)
St Andrew's CE Primary School, North Weald

The School Field

In the summer it's lovely and hot, it makes us feel happy
Spring flowers are growing all around
The grass is green, the trees tall and waving
Lots of playing children, fun for them all
Beautiful butterflies playing in the blue sky
Red squirrels climbing way up high.

Charlotte Jones (9)
St Andrew's CE Primary School, North Weald

Meg

She runs as fast as a tornado
Though she is cute and cuddly
She gets very dirty on walks
She is as small as an ant
When you give her a treat she eats it
Who is it?
It's *Meg* the Jack Russell.

Thomas Saye (9)
St Andrew's CE Primary School, North Weald

Disco

Leaving school, feeling extremely boisterous
Saying goodbye to my friends
Saying, 'See you at the disco,'
Getting my football kit and my groovy shoes on
Getting my coat on
Looking for some spare change to pay for the disco
Jogging to school
Warming my legs up for the dancing
Seeing my friends in groovy outfits and chatting to them
Dancing with my friends
Getting into the groove and eating food.

Ben Bailey (8)
St Andrew's CE Primary School, North Weald

Moment

In the jungle
Not an animal around
All was dark
Suddenly
The sun peeped through
Animals came out
Never hid away again
Not even a mouse.

Chloe West (8)
St Andrew's CE Primary School, North Weald

Moment

Three little starving puppies
Very, very wet
Scratching on a door
Hoping to be cared for.

Harry Docking (8)
St Andrew's CE Primary School, North Weald

Disco

I am leaving school
I am very excited
Mum has got new clothes for me
I am walking back again
I see my friends
They have smart clothes
We have all different music to dance to
There was a raffle
And I won the best prize
Then I went home.

Jordan Smith (7)
St Andrew's CE Primary School, North Weald

Monkeys

M onkeys and gorillas and
O rang-utans are all apes
N o swinging in the cage
K ind, yet vicious in the wild
E xciting to watch them
Y ou will never catch them
S afe and sound in the jungle for now.

Lewis King (10)
St Andrew's CE Primary School, North Weald

Moment

Among the gutters
And dustbin lids
A sudden scream
From a car
It stopped
A man was hurt
Whiplash!

Richard Bailey (7)
St Andrew's CE Primary School, North Weald

Disco

Bell rang!
Home I ran
I sang and sang disco!
Oh yeah!
Home I got, upstairs I ran
Got dressed in the latest disco, yeah.
Walked to school
Saw my friends
Saw their clothes
Couldn't believe my eyes
Danced for ages
Got worn out
Dad came all the way
He took me home.

Amy Morris (8)
St Andrew's CE Primary School, North Weald

Nissan Skyline

N ice car with NOS
I nteresting vinyl
S peakers in the truck
S uperfast car
A cceleration
N OS

S poiler
K eys
Y ou have got specially made seats
L ittle lights
I nteresting rims
N eons glowing
E xciting ride.

Sam Barker (10)
St Andrew's CE Primary School, North Weald

Sam, Sam, Still Contrary
(Inspired by 'Sam, Sam, Quite Contrary' by Chrissie Gittins)

Sam, Sam still contrary
does no work
but dresses as a fairy

Sam, Sam still contrary
married Suzannah
forgot about Mary

Sam, Sam still contrary
bought a balloon
and went all airy

Sam, Sam still contrary
meant to kiss Suzannah
but kissed his canary

Sam, Sam still contrary
bought a wig
and went all hairy!

Iona Manley (9)
St Teresa's RC Primary School, Colchester

The Horrible Brother

I got out of bed and bumped my head
And fell down the ladder
I kicked the cat
And called my brother fat
And he got even madder
I ran round the house and saw a mouse
And my brother got even sadder
I broke the table
And I sat in a stable and I got even sadder
And I found a rhyme but I seem to do it all the time.

Daniel O'Reilly (9)
St Teresa's RC Primary School, Colchester

A Tsunami

Under the waves, ready to pounce,
No one knows anything is going to happen.
The water weighs no more than an ounce,
God save them, amen.

When it pounces it's a whole new force,
People get nervous because of the lull.
The water's ten times the speed of a horse,
Wrecking boats by smashing through the hull.

Crashing into land, drowning loads of people,
Separating children from their parents.
The water is very lethal,
The wave dismantling a piece of fence.

When it finishes, the destruction is colossal,
People homeless and sad.
The wave wipes away every fossil,
No one in this world is glad.

Glenn Wheeler (9)
St Teresa's RC Primary School, Colchester

The Witch

The witch as scary as can be
When you look at her you scream
When she mixes her potions
She makes lots of scary motions.

Her raven stands on a pole
Standing there it caws and caws
The cat looks up all scary and fierce as can be
She'll scratch, she'll bite, she'll do anything she wants to.

The witch has lice-covered hair
Her clothes as black as pitch-black
She's covered in warts
You would not want to feel one
She's got spiders in her hair and cobwebs in her teeth.

Anna Bishop (9)
St Teresa's RC Primary School, Colchester

Winter Is Over

Winter is over, not very funny
Now I'm staying in it's sunny
My snowmen are starting to melt
You wouldn't know how I felt.

I went to school to see my friend
We played table football and I had to defend.
Went outside and had a fight
I made him bleed with a killing bite
He went to hospital and he had rabies
He saw his mum having babies.

Alfie Payne (9)
St Teresa's RC Primary School, Colchester

A Snowy Day

The alarm was a troll beating me out of bed
I ran to the window and said,
'Mum, Dad, it's snowing outside
Can I get my sleigh and slide?'

I went for a ride, got a wet behind
So my mum got very unkind
Crashed into the step, flew into the door
Got snow all over the kitchen floor.

Charyl Spencer (10)
St Teresa's RC Primary School, Colchester

Snakes

Snakes are as colourful as a flower
And have lots of markings as clear as a red ruby
Some are poisonous, some are not
But most are strong and deadly
When they hunt they are as fast as a jaguar
Hunting for his prey and as clever as an eagle hunting for its prey.

Conor Culhane (10)
St Teresa's RC Primary School, Colchester

The Witch

She has a cat
That always snorts
She has a bat
With lots of warts
He face is green
She hates the queen
That is why she normally travels at night.

She has nasty nails
Her tricks normally fail
Although they fail, she is actually really mean,
But she has a fear, that fear may be orange, orange beans
Still her pets are stranger
They live in a manger
And have to cope with the wicked villain's team.

She has freckles on her toes
And a very crooked nose
Her broomstick smells bad
So the neighbours go mad
She wears a long, black robe
Since that's all she has in her wardrobe.

Keshini Gooneratne (10)
St Teresa's RC Primary School, Colchester

A Summer's Day

There's a lot of kids splashing in the sea
I had to stay in for cookie robbery.

Finally, let out in a muddle
I was so dizzy I fell in a puddle.

I fell in the sea with a crash and a bang
Because some guys pushed me, I think it was a gang.

All this happened in one day
So I don't think I'll come out to play.

Ben Brown (10)
St Teresa's RC Primary School, Colchester

Sunday Morning Football Match

It was Sunday morn
I woke up with the dawn
I had a football match
I'm a goalie and can catch.

I spring out of bed
And then I got my lucky ted
I got in a very bad fit
Because I lost my orange kit.

I peeked out of the door
And then I surely saw
A slippery, slidy, snowy sight
It gave me quite a fright.

I finally found my kit
And then the whole room lit
I slipped on the ice
That wasn't very nice.

I finally got to the football game
And said, 'Come on we're doing lame.'
And since I was in goal
I was on a great big roll.

The score was one all
And then we got the ball
I thought it was very fun
Because we won 2-1.

Daniel Congdon (9)
St Teresa's RC Primary School, Colchester

The Witch

She is so fat just like her cat
She never knows when to stop
She flies on her broom, into her tomb
There goes the queen of doom.

Abigail Payne (9)
St Teresa's RC Primary School, Colchester

The Zoo Zoo Monster

The Zoo Zoo monster from Mars
Loves to eat people and plants
Has five eyes and has four legs
Shakes people until they're dead.

The Zoo Zoo monster has lots of fingers and toes
He has two hundred of each you know
It'll pick you up and snap you in half
When he's eaten you, he'll have a laugh.

It lives in an old house made of wood
He goes into the town disguised with a hood
The Zoo Zoo monster is very cruel
So watch out all of you!

John Deasy (10)
St Teresa's RC Primary School, Colchester

The Death Of An Ugly Queen!

The queen she was quite chubby
She never bathed so she was grubby
Good thing she died
Nobody cried
She really was quite stubby.

Katie Clements (9)
St Teresa's RC Primary School, Colchester

Giants

The cave makes noises like a big *bang*
- *Bang* from a gun
And any man that comes near,
They will get hanged.
The weapons are as sharp as T-rex teeth
And the gold treasure is beneath.

Jack Lugar (9)
St Teresa's RC Primary School, Colchester

Mr Knockerbocker

Mr Knockerbocker is the maddest,
If something is wrong then he's the saddest,
He has his head in the clouds night and day,
If you upset him, you'll have to pay!

He has the clocks an hour late
And no wheels on a roller-skate,
He tries his hardest, poor lad,
But you have to admit, he's barking mad!

Alex Partner (10)
St Teresa's RC Primary School, Colchester

Chocolate

Crunchy, crispy, creamy chocolate
Munchy, milky, melting chocolate
Lots of different kinds of chocolate
Yummy in my tummy!

Soft, sticky, sweet chocolate
Warm, welcoming, wonderful chocolate
Thank you God for all the chocolate
It's better than my mummy!

Paola Williams (9)
St Teresa's RC Primary School, Colchester

Year 5

They gurgle, splutter, scream and shout,
The teacher's always shrieking, 'Out!'
They always love a food fight
To chuck the grub with all their might.

The teacher's losing all control
Head teacher always on patrol
You tell them off, they lose the plot
Year 5, they are a terrible lot!

Ruth Chanarin (9)
St Teresa's RC Primary School, Colchester

The Witch

She has a great big wart
And a nasty snort
Her face is green
She's really mean
And she has no friends at all.

Her pets are cruel
She's such a fool
The cat it barks!
And the bat leaves marks
On every single wall.

She has a nasty smile
Because she is a crocodile
She is extremely hairy
And very scary
She is never nice.

She has a pointy nose
And spots on her toes
She's also very creepy
And never ever sleepy.

Rachel Cresswell (9)
St Teresa's RC Primary School, Colchester

Weather

The weather is a funny clown
It changes every day
One day it is hot
One day it is cold
And when it's raining we all run away!

The weather is hot
And the sun is out
And we all go to the beach
To swim in the sea
In the salty deep blue sea.

Bradley Collins (10)
St Teresa's RC Primary School, Colchester

Mr Hackenbacker!

Mr Hackenbacker,
Such a stupid man,
He loves to chatter
And his real name's Stan!

He gets up every morning,
His bath overflows,
Always forever yawning
In his out of fashion clothes!

Getting in the car,
There's always a crash,
Back home for tea,
Bangers and mash!

He's getting a new job, hooray,
Oh no, it's a complete disaster,
He's a decorator you see,
He can't apply plaster!

You'd know him if you met him,
Hackenbackers are tall,
He hasn't got any hair on his head,
I swear it, none at all!

Christine Quilty (10)
St Teresa's RC Primary School, Colchester

Chocolate

The best of all is white,
So I drool over the sight
But after all it's night
So I can't take a bite.

Second of all is dark,
All cold and chewy like bark
So big like a horrible shark
It's also hard so have a lark.

Benjamin Woods (10)
St Teresa's RC Primary School, Colchester

Betty And The Tiger

There once was a girl called Betty
She really adored spaghetti
Her hair was quite gold
She was ten-years old.

One day Betty was walking down to the pool
She tried to look really cool
Then a tiger jumped out, what a figure
Betty said, 'Hello, I'll call you Tigger.'

Betty said, 'You're a pretty big cat.'
She scratched his belly and said, 'Look at that.'
The tiger gave a thunderous roar
The girl said, 'Would you like a tour?'

The girl said, 'Come home,
Do not worry, I'm on my own.'
She took him through the front door
And sat him on the velvet floor.

The tiger said, 'Take me home
I feel so alone.'
'Do you want to go back to the zoo?'
'I don't know what to do.'

She said, 'There's only one thing to do
I've got to take you back to the zoo.'
She took him to a friendly man
He said, 'Oh I'll call him Fran.'

The tiger said, 'Thank you Betty
One day I'll come back and try your spaghetti.'

Chloe Williams (10)
St Teresa's RC Primary School, Colchester

The Monkey

In the rainforest, it was a sunny day
A monkey was swinging up high
All was calm and it looked like a bay
The monkey looked like it was flying by.

Max monkey tumbled into a lake
Where he met his friend, Carl crocodile
He asked, 'Would you like a piece of cake?'
Max looked behind and saw a massive pile.

Max jumped out and went on land
It was so hot, it was like an oven
He met his friend Sam snail with a wristband
But ran and hid near a cavern.

The cavern made a terrible spell
That caused rain and a thunderstorm
The rainforest now looked like hell
So Max jumped into a tree
And thanked God that it wasn't a snowstorm.

Max was jumping and running through the trees
Until he stopped, like a solid object lying around
He was madly wobbling his knees
When suddenly a bolt hit the branch
And sent Max hurtling to the ground.
He was dead!

William Jennings (10)
St Teresa's RC Primary School, Colchester

A Riddle

My spots are holes out of the night sky,
All of my friends have not eaten a single fly,
My fur is soft silk, smooth velvet,
Yet some people call me a mangy mutt,
I'm as friendly as your best friend,
Yet I can be fierce to the bitter end.
What am I?

Rebecca Lenihan (10)
St Teresa's RC Primary School, Colchester

Oh No!

Oh no, I'm late for school
Oh no, I'm in the swimming pool
Oh no, I'm all but wet
Oh yes, the sun has set.

Oh no, it's a dull, boring day
I wish I could play
This happens every other night
Oh good, my house is in sight.

All right, I'm fed up of this
I'm going home to watch 'The Brits'.
Sitting by the nice warm fire
Oh no, I've got a punctured tyre.

Joe Campe (9)
St Teresa's RC Primary School, Colchester

My First Goal

I got the ball that's really cool
It's at my feet, that's neat,
Someone going for a hack, it's going to be a smack
I'm going fast, I'm a blast.

There's a player, is he a good lay-er?
We're 1-0 down, I've got a frown.
We scored a goal, we have control
I'm going for a header, that's really clever.

There's a pole, it is the goal
There's the keeper, his name is Peter
If I don't score, it will be poor
I've scored, I've scored.

Nicollas Campbell (9)
St Teresa's RC Primary School, Colchester

The Cave

The cave is dark and gloomy, with bats as black as pitch
Dead fish scattered everywhere
The sound of heavy breathing echoing through the cave
Smoke all around.

At the heart of the dread cave lies a dragon as red, as red as blood
Ashes everywhere you go
Skeletons all grey and burnt.

Ice-cold water with dead bats inside
Blue saliva everywhere
Blood all over the ceiling which drips onto the floor.

James Chambers (9)
St Teresa's RC Primary School, Colchester

Friends

Some people have lots of friends, some people have one,
But if you're unlucky, you may have none,
Some friends are fat, some friends are slim,
Some friends are smart, while others are dim.

Some friends are boring, some friends are fun,
Some friends walk and some friends run,
Some friends are white, some friends are brown,
But if they're a different colour, don't give them a frown.

Sophie Wilcocks (9)
St Teresa's RC Primary School, Colchester

Gordon Brown

Gordon Brown, Gordon Brown
Always seems to wear a frown
He opens his box on Budget Day
And tells us what taxes we have to pay.

Ryan Jackson (10)
The Daiglen School

My Dog Missy

Floor soaker
Fast drinker
Cat hater
Food cruncher
Brilliant footballer
Plant eater
Toy lover
TV watcher
Finger biter
Toe nibbler.

Jacob Hopkins (10)
The Daiglen School

Cheetah

Fast runner
Wicked winner
Bad loser
Great growler
Long snoozer
Far jumper
Cub producer
Deer killer
Brilliant cheater.

Jason Chan (10)
The Daiglen School

Old Pensioner

There was a very old man from East Ham
Who in World War II ate awful Spam
Now he collects his pension
And stands up to attention
To people who are fighting for ham.

Sam Winter (11)
The Daiglen School

George Best

Big drinker
Huge boozer
Woman abuser
Football player
Great striker
Ball controller
Defence beater
Goal scorer
Irish blighter
Getting older
Much iller
Second liver.

Sam Dooley (10)
The Daiglen School

Winter

Robins fly
Across the sky
As the rivers flow
As the snow
Crashes on the ground
There is no sound
The sun goes up
As the snow goes down.

Max Goreham (8)
The Daiglen School

The Gazoo Playing Bird

There was once a bird from the zoo
Who loved to play the gazoo
Got stuck in a tree
Was stung by a bee
And started to cry, 'Boo-hoo!'

Roshan Sukeerathan (10)
The Daiglen School

A Nice Snowy Day

It is beginning to snow
The ice is so slippery
I say, 'Come on let's go.'
I hate it when the sun comes out
But when it snows I love to shout
I hate it when the snow goes away
But since the snow is here, let's play
Snow is great
I will have snowball fights with my mate
I'll make a snowman
And play with my gran.

Connor Marcelis (8)
The Daiglen School

The Kangaroo

There once was a kangaroo
Who walked down the avenue
He jumped on Sam
And ate all his ham
So Sam cried and said, 'Boo-hoo!'

Chirage Valera (10)
The Daiglen School

A Snowy Day

Snow is dropping from the cold air
Winter is here
People put on their boots and have a blast
Frozen lakes in the park
Snowflakes have been falling
Icicles hang from frozen roofs
Winter is here.

Charlie Pigrome (8)
The Daiglen School

Peregrine Falcon

Great flyer
Sky glider
Prey hunter
Fast mover
Superb sighter
Rapid slayer
Head twister
Animal charger
Foe killer
Bird eater
Record breaker
Speed master
Never loser
Tree liver
Sight winner.

Nigel Ip (10)
The Daiglen School

Rain And Storm

A storm makes a banging sound
Soon it starts raining so people rush home
Nobody is at the park
Water is pattering on the roofs.

The storm is roaring
Rain splashes on people's faces
The cars are soaking
The storm makes the babies cry.

People have coats on
People have umbrellas up
People put on their fires
But tomorrow it will be sunny.

Jake Lewis (7)
The Daiglen School

Snow

It's cold and freezing
It's really white
It's extremely bright
It covers the ground.

It's especially slippery
And it causes delays
It moves quickly
It freezes water.

We like to play in the snow
I definitely know
You can make many things
This is why I like the snow.

Samuel Meah (8)
The Daiglen School

Snow And Ice

Roads become dangerous
Children get their sledges
They go to the hills
And sled past the hedges.

Rain turns to snow and ice
Icicles hang from the rooftop
The windows have icicles too
Winter never seems to stop.

Now it is spring
The snow and ice thaw out
Soon it will be Easter
And a chocolate bout!

Harrison Jones (8)
The Daiglen School

Snow

It is fun to play with
It is cold
It is on your roof
It is on your window
It is on your car
It comes in a season
You can throw it on someone
You can play snowballs
You can ski on the high mountains
Snow is white
Snow is bright.

Zain Rana (7)
The Daiglen School

Snow

S now is smooth and shiny
N ow I watch my snowman melt
O n the fields I play
W hen the sun comes out, I watch the snow go away
M aking snowballs is really fun
A nd children crack ice to make the rivers flow
N ever wear a T-shirt in the snow.

Joe Garland (8)
The Daiglen School

Ali

There once was a man called Ali
Who couldn't even do a tally
He fell off a tree
Eating a bumblebee
And blamed it on his daughter Sally.

Ali Siddiqui (10)
The Daiglen School

Liar, Liar

Early last Monday I found I could lie,
So I hopped on our roof and threw a big pie,
But no one was hit or taken aback,
Mum simply called, 'Come down, let me give you a smack!'

At night on Monday, I put a rat in Mum's bed,
I put it in a frightening place, right near her head,
When she got into her bed, she rolled over,
Instead of screaming, she threw it up over Rover!

On the following morning I got Dad's hat,
I threw a paint ball, it went *splat*,
Our cat Romer went into a coma,
Then got buried next to the mower.

In the end I got found out, sneaking about,
They asked what I was doing,
I told them the truth,
That I was going to play a prank on Ruth.

William Reynolds (10)
Tolleshunt D'Arcy St Nicholas CE Primary School

In the Playground

Chatting children
Slapping of a skipping rope hitting the ground
Boys kick the football with a thud
Bang, it hits a girl and pushes her in the mud.

Children's laughter fills the air
Sweetly singing birds swoop down gently landing
Rubbish softly flying through the air.

Beautiful flowers on swishing, swaying grass
Tall trees rustling
Sun beaming down on us
The bell at the end of playtime
Ding, ding, I enjoy playtime.

Zoe Rigby (9)
Tolleshunt D'Arcy St Nicholas CE Primary School

What Will Become Of The Playground?

Although it's strange, I have to say,
The playground is my friend,
And every night I wonder
If its life shall come to an end.

The way that it is treated
Is unfair in every way -
The evil things they do to it,
Each and every day.

Like using it for battles,
Blood left on the floor.
Litter scattered haphazardly -
Increasing more and more.

Rebels drawing on the walls,
Graffiti here and there,
It could grow, cover the place,
Yet no one seems to care.

I pity my mate the playground,
But others couldn't care less.
If they don't stop and think sometime,
My buddy will just be a mess.

Josh Bolding (11)
Tolleshunt D'Arcy St Nicholas CE Primary School

The Forest Poem

Woodpeckers drilling on the tree, when the trees are blowing in
                                                                           the wind
Birds singing
Tortoises walking slowly on the ground
Foxes sniffing by the tree, waiting for food to eat
Rabbits jumping quietly
So the fox does not hear them
They come out every year
Come and see what they can do to you.

Grace Goodman (9)
Tolleshunt D'Arcy St Nicholas CE Primary School

Playground

Skipping ropes swinging
Balls flying
Children crying
Basketballs bouncing
Birds singing
Teachers shouting
Bells ringing
Children playing
Trees rustling
Swings swinging.

Clare Lofthouse (8)
Tolleshunt D'Arcy St Nicholas CE Primary School

Sounds

Birds singing in the trees,
Waterfalls splash all around,
Woodpeckers drilling through the trees,
Blistering winds blowing the trees,
Basketballs bouncing,
Footballs flying,
Seagulls swooping down to pick up food.

Harry Wakefield (8)
Tolleshunt D'Arcy St Nicholas CE Primary School

My House

In my house I can hear . . .
Windows flapping
Keys turning
Dogs barking
Doors creaking
This is my house.

Ryan Bentley (8)
Tolleshunt D'Arcy St Nicholas CE Primary School

Looking Through The Window

I can see a calm river by a pretty meadow.
It has buttercups and daisies.
I can hear the river and the wind blows in the grass.
I feel like a special girl
And the animals feel special like me.
I like animals because they are nice.
All kinds of animals.
I love God,
The animals love God as well.

Chloe Double (8)
Tolleshunt D'Arcy St Nicholas CE Primary School

Pirate

Old Blackbeard,
he was a terrible man.
He sailed the seven seas,
and stole from all the land.
He got scabs and bruises from all his fights.
He's lucky someone didn't put out his lights.
Don't bump into him on a dark night,
because he will give you a big fright.

James Baker (9)
Tolleshunt D'Arcy St Nicholas CE Primary School

Looking Through The Window

I can see a meadow,
A sea of butterflies.
The sun is setting.
I can hear a river
And the fish diving.
I feel very relaxed.

Tom Delderfield (8)
Tolleshunt D'Arcy St Nicholas CE Primary School

Hypnotised

I tiptoe out of the grass shining
Like the king has dressed every blade,
Owls swooping to catch their prey,
The gate creaks,
I freeze
Scared I am
I walk down the cold path
A creature in the moonlight
What happens?
I pray I never find out.

Sarah Harris (8)
Tolleshunt D'Arcy St Nicholas CE Primary School

In The Woods

Blackbirds are singing everywhere,
Green apples tumble off rustling trees,
Speeding waterfalls are splashing all over the stony ground,
Foxes sniffing amongst the trees waiting, waiting to get rabbits,
Winds are heavily blowing,
Everyone come and join in the fun!

Jessica Poulter (9)
Tolleshunt D'Arcy St Nicholas CE Primary School

Stormy City

As I enter the stormy city, cracks of thunder I hear.
Bolts of lightning flash before my eyes.
Smell of smoke from a struck-down tree alerts me.
I climb over a rough, hot, tall, fallen tree.
I sit by a fire, the sight warms my heart.
As I exit the stormy city (cracks of thunder I hear).

William Skelton (9)
Tolleshunt D'Arcy St Nicholas CE Primary School

Our Playground

Our playground holds lots of people
Some from France and one from Constantinople
There's old Jonny, he's always in a fight
Wouldn't want to be his mother tonight
Some people like me some people don't
The best thing is when Teachy over there can't find his coat
(We hide it in our janitor's cupboard.)
The cry of the ravens makes me shudder
The playground is full of fun
A rest from the scratching of pencils
Frantically trying to get work done
So if you were even to pass by our school
Come in to our playground and play football.

Sam Armstrong (11)
Tolleshunt D'Arcy St Nicholas CE Primary School

Looking Through The Window

I can see a lovely lake in the meadow
And a tortoise.
Birds singing.
I feel the love of my mum and dad in my heart.

Sarah King (7)
Tolleshunt D'Arcy St Nicholas CE Primary School

In The Garden

Flowers swaying in the breeze
Trees and fleas jumping up and down.
The smell of burgers in the wind are ghosts in the air.
Dogs barking, birds singing and going tweet in the garden.

George Basham (9)
Tolleshunt D'Arcy St Nicholas CE Primary School

Looking Through The Window

I can see a pond
And there is grass round it.
Lovely colourful buttercups and daffodils
And I can see a tortoise.
Blue-white clouds,
Birds and pretty butterflies.
I can hear seagulls singing
And the trees rustling.
You can hear the wind.
I can feel the wind
And I can feel the joy,
I feel joyful.

Alice Moore (7)
Tolleshunt D'Arcy St Nicholas CE Primary School

Looking Through The Window

I can see pretty green grass.
I hope this dream will last.
There is a beautiful park with shiny bark.
I can glide.
I can see some monkey bars.
I can see toy cars.
I can hear the wind blowing on my hand.
I can hear my next-door neighbour's band.

Emmie Bolding (8)
Tolleshunt D'Arcy St Nicholas CE Primary School

Things In The Playground

Thumping of little girls jumping over skipping ropes.
The hollow sound of boys kicking footballs.
Stampeding children running this way and that.
Basketballs bouncing out of control.
At the ringing of the bell everything is still and silent.

Maya Tucker (9)
Tolleshunt D'Arcy St Nicholas CE Primary School

Lost In The Woods!

I am scared, scared. I am all the foxes howling loudly,
Birds squawking fiercely,
The smell of fragrant mint leaves,
Splashing waterfalls splatter madly,
Sound of thumping water, green ivy leaves crawling round the trees,
Blistering, blowing winds jumpily sway over the crispy, damp leaves,
Woodpeckers drill against the wood on the trees,
How wonderful it is for us to spy on many amazing creatures.

Kristie Smith (9)
Tolleshunt D'Arcy St Nicholas CE Primary School

The Ghost

My window was open,
The trees were rustling,
It was like I could see something,
It was like a ghost.
It had horns,
It came closer,
It was the bogeyman
And he crumpled me
In his bogey embrace.

Drew Talbot (9)
Tolleshunt D'Arcy St Nicholas CE Primary School

Looking Through The Window

I can see my house. My garden.
Birds sitting on the chimney.
Mum's hanging washing out.
I can hear birds squawking
And children talking.
I feel happy. It's a great house.
It's a great garden.

George Davison (7)
Tolleshunt D'Arcy St Nicholas CE Primary School

The Playground

On the playground everyone's running,
Until someone turns very cunning,
And trips the first one to the ground,
Then chaos sweeps all around.

People running, bashing, crashing,
Pushing, shoving, shouting, yelling.
No one knows just where they are,
But soon comes the head's car.

Silence spreads through the flock,
As they slowly make their way back under the lock.
So be careful on the playground,
It's not safe, look around!

Stay inside that's my advice,
Or you'll get bashed more than twice!

Amy Harrison (9)
Tolleshunt D'Arcy St Nicholas CE Primary School

In The Playground

Rubbish floating around the playground.
Children crying.
Football bouncing.
Skipping ropes left on the ground.
Children on the climbing frame.

Ashley Hawkes (9)
Tolleshunt D'Arcy St Nicholas CE Primary School

Looking Through The Window

A blue lake with fish in.
Animals running around.
Birds singing, trees rustling.
Breeze, wind.

Christopher Lewis (8)
Tolleshunt D'Arcy St Nicholas CE Primary School

Playground

In the playground there is lots of noise,
Between all the students; girls and boys,
Some are standing in the corners talking,
Others are sitting on the benches sulking.

On the playground there are some fights,
Between people who think they're standing up for their rights,
They don't seem to care about anyone else,
Except their friends or themselves.

On the playground when the bell rings,
Everyone bustles around for their things,
You can see people running around,
That's what happens on our playground.

Katie Lofthouse (11)
Tolleshunt D'Arcy St Nicholas CE Primary School

Looking Through The Window

I can see a river,
Passing slowly by.
Blue like the sky.
I can hear a boat.
It's a fast boat.
I wonder where it's going.

Brendan Bush (7)
Tolleshunt D'Arcy St Nicholas CE Primary School

Darkness

In the dark world, people moving,
Mice squeaking,
Owls swiftly gliding in the moonlight.
All stars twinkling bright.
As dark as coal and as quiet as light.

Ben Rees (9)
Tolleshunt D'Arcy St Nicholas CE Primary School

Looking Through The Window

I can see some trees and a pair of eyes,
A question mark, a castle, Pokémon
And a frog combined with a rabbit.
I can hear the roar of a tiger.
I can feel God's love in me.

Edward Baker (7)
Tolleshunt D'Arcy St Nicholas CE Primary School

Looking Through The Window

I can see a calm and gentle river,
With sparkling fish
And a meadow with sheep in white curls.
I can hear trees rustling in the air.
I can feel the breezy hotness of the sun.

Katie Peaker (7)
Tolleshunt D'Arcy St Nicholas CE Primary School

Looking Through The Window

I can see a castle with trees and birds.
I can hear a bird singing in the wind
And whistling in the breeze.
I feel dreamy.

Amy Hawkes (7)
Tolleshunt D'Arcy St Nicholas CE Primary School

Looking Through The Window

A jumping frog, castle and a field.
There are lots of flowers.
The frog croaks at the guns on the castle.
I feel joyful.

Jack Garrett (7)
Tolleshunt D'Arcy St Nicholas CE Primary School

Looking Through The Window

I can see a lake,
A tyre on a tree.
I can hear a hum
From a hummingbird.
Warm.

Kelly Bentley (7)
Tolleshunt D'Arcy St Nicholas CE Primary School

Looking Through The Window

Wet, glittery grass.
Even concrete shines with brightness.
I hear the wind soothe and calm.
I feel happy, the sun is bright,
Lovely wild animals playing around.

Sam Harris (8)
Tolleshunt D'Arcy St Nicholas CE Primary School

Looking Through The Window

A lovely seaside with birds, bushes and sand.
I can hear the sea rustling,
Birds singing, people talking and wind blowing.
I feel the wind blowing in my hair.

Alice Pettican (8)
Tolleshunt D'Arcy St Nicholas CE Primary School

Looking Through The Window

Green trees swishing side to side
And colourful birds singing in the wind.
The trees showing off their lovely coats.
The freedoms of God's life.

Stacey Dolby (8)
Tolleshunt D'Arcy St Nicholas CE Primary School

Looking Through The Window

I can see a river.
I can see a flock of birds.
I can see a kangaroo.
I can see poppies and daisies,
Pine trees and tropical trees.
I can hear birds singing.
I can hear the river sploshing.
I can hear pine trees and tropical trees
That sway in the breeze.
I feel fury.

Joshua Searles (7)
Tolleshunt D'Arcy St Nicholas CE Primary School

Looking Through The Window

A butterfly swoops in swirls,
Like a beautiful pearl
In the light of the world.
He spreads colours for others.
I hear the swoop of wings.
I feel love.

India Rigby (7)
Tolleshunt D'Arcy St Nicholas CE Primary School

My Mum

My mum is amazing,
She buys me cards and food.
If I didn't have a mum,
I would be very sad
But they can be horrible.

Frederick Phillips (8)
Tolleshunt D'Arcy St Nicholas CE Primary School

The Seasons Of The Playground

Whoosh! came the north-east wind
Showing that winter is near
It'll be very cold I'm sure
But it doesn't matter about me.

Now I can see the flowers popping up
Showing it must be spring
I'll look so beautiful and splendid
It's natural for the time of year.

It's summer and I am forgotten
The grass is what they want now
I try to be very welcoming.

Autumn brings rain and inside play
I'm wishing for spring
Where I'll look good and inviting
And children will come to me.

Ben Knights (10)
Tolleshunt D'Arcy St Nicholas CE Primary School

The Playground Through The Seasons

Spring, no one makes a sound. From the classroom,
children watch blossom fall to the floor of the playground.

In the playground there is a warm summer's breeze
and you can hear birds singing in the trees.

Autumn, no one makes a sound.
Leaves flutter around the floor of the playground.

In the playground winter brings snow.
Little children don't know where to go.

The seasons of the playground differ a lot.
I love the playground, others do not.

Summer Phillips (10)
Tolleshunt D'Arcy St Nicholas CE Primary School

Playground Fight

Friend and foe meet,
Where the grass is trimmed neat
And is ruled by the King of the Hares.

The crowd starts to cheer,
The other side jeers,
When the boys begin to fight.

Foot and fist fly,
All because of a lie,
That was told in the stuffy classroom.

The bell starts to ring
And children run in,
But the boys just carry on fighting.

And 5 minutes later,
The head, Mrs Sayter,
Comes rushing out in a rage.

The boys are dragged in,
Aware of their sin,
Awaiting their final doom.

The parents are told,
Of the boys who were bold
And fought in the middle of playtime.

Adam Dyster (11)
Tolleshunt D'Arcy St Nicholas CE Primary School